Roots

D1147226

A Play

Arnold Wesker

Samuel French – London
New York – Sydney – Toronto – Hollywood

ISBN 0 573 11377 7

Printed in Great Britain by
Redwood Books, Trowbridge, Wiltshire

Roots

This play was first produced at the Belgrade Theatre, Coventry, on 25th May 1959, and subsequently by the English Stage Company, with the Belgrade, Theatre Company, at the Royal Court Theatre, London, on 30th June, 1959, with the following cast:

JENNY BEALES	..	..	..	..	..	..	*Patsy Byrne*
JIMMY BEALES	..	..	..	..	..	..	*Charles Kay*
BEATIE BRYANT	..	..	..	..	..	..	*Joan Plowright*
STAN MANN ..	..	..	..	..	..	..	*Patrick O'Connell*
MRS. BRYANT	..	..	..	..	..	..	*Gwen Nelson*
MR. BRYANT ..	..	..	..	..	..	..	*Jack Rodney*
MR. HEALEY ..	..	..	..	..	..	..	*Richard Martin*
FRANKIE BRYANT	..	..	..	..	..	..	*Alan Howard*
PEARL BRYANT	..	..	..	..	..	..	*Brenda Peters*

The play was directed by JOHN DEXTER *with décor by*
JOCELYN HERBERT

ACT ONE
An isolated cottage in Norfolk, the house of the Beales'.

ACT TWO
SCENE 1. The kitchen at the cottage of Mr. and Mrs. Bryant. Two days later.
SCENE 2. The same. Two hours later.

ACT THREE
The front room of the Bryants' cottage. Two weeks later.

No character in this play is intended to portray any specific person, alive or dead.

Running time of this play, excluding intervals, is approximately one hour and forty minutes.

PRODUCTION NOTE

THIS play deals, fundamentally, with the problem of communication, or the lack of it. Because the people it concerns have little knowledge of the power and use of words, of language, they can be imposed on and cheated, are unable to develop and inadequate to deal with a crisis even when it occurs in their own intimate circle. They are the gullible prey of catch-penny advertisers and purveyors of cheap shoddy goods, whether for body or mind. They are not unhappy. They have no feeling of self-pity: it might be better if they had and it led to a discontent which caused them to pull themselves out of their pleasant rut, their easy acceptance of a life which is so much poorer than it might be. The author offers no easy solution to a problem which may well have none, merely leaving us with a ray of hope that here and there one of them may become, in all the word implies, "articulate". He presents his characters without sentiment, almost harshly, but with all the deeper sympathy and understanding because of his uncompromising approach.

The cast is rich in acting opportunites. First and foremost Beatie—a long and exacting part making considerable demands on the player, but fully repaying all the time and work spent on it. Beatie overflows with health, vigour and, above all, enthusiasm. It is this, more than any real superiority of intelligence, which forms the contrast to her more stolid and undemonstrative family. We feel that she has broken through some boundary in which they are still enclosed. It is these qualities also which prevent her from any appearance of patronage in her attitude to them. She never talks down to them, never bosses them about even when, in the first act, she starts to clean up Jenny's house. She has made, through Ronnie, a wonderful discovery—the power of language and all it entails—and with all her heart she longs to pass this on to her own people. Her enthusiasm enables us to see him through her eyes, and perhaps, unconsciously, through eyes rather more critical than her own. Her collapse on hearing of her betrayal is short-lived. Ronnie may have let her down but he has, though with little credit to himself, left her a legacy which will transform her life.

Jenny is a pleasant-natured, easy-going young housewife. She is not a sloven. If her house is an untidy mess, this is because she simply has not the time to get around to cleaning it up. She accepts life as she finds it, as she no doubt accepted her illegitimate baby, without rancour. Her references to the favoured treatment her sister used to receive when they were children are statements of fact rather than expressions of past resentment. Her rather pathetic pride in her bread baking perhaps affords us a glimpse of a creative impulse which in different circumstances might have developed, but she is already firmly settled in the family groove and it will take more than speeches from Beatie to dig her out of it.

Jimmy appears a wholy unexceptionable (and unexceptional) young workman, who earns his wage and looks after his family, but he has probably never had an original thought in his head, and his pride in his uniform, together with his unthinking acceptance of any orders he may receive while wearing it, suggests less desirable attributes. He would be ready, one feels, to swallow any slogan rather than worry out the purpose behind it and one can picture him in a pre-war Germany proudly displaying a swastika on his sleeve.

Mrs. Bryant is a devastatingly true portrait of a type of woman most of us come across at one time or another. She may in this instance talk with a Norfolk accent but her prototypes, allowing for regional differences, may be met with anywhere. The part is a magnificent one but calling for careful handling and discipline. It must never degenerate into caricature or be played for the cheap laugh.

Mr. Bryant, in contrast to his wife who, narrow and uninformed though she may be, has at least a character which can make itself felt, is a small man in every way, physically, mentally and spiritually. Even his meanness is a small one. Insignificant and feckless, complaining about his work conditions and at the same time unable to bother opening "that old thing" the Union Magazine—he yet fathered Beatie—who breaks free.

The smaller parts, Stan Mann, Mr. Healy, Frank and Pearl, are written, and should be played, with as much subtlety and truth as the others.

Stan Mann might be regarded as the end product of the system— placidly undergoing in public the indignities of senility, lost in an allegedly happier past like any elderly West End club bore, collapsing at last in a heap almost undistinguishable, one feels, from the earth close to which he has lived and worked.

Frank Bryant is a pleasant enough young man with a line in cheap wit which, excusable now, may in time turn him into a prize bore, as his pretty, opinionated wife may finish up an embittered nagger. One feels that it is at their gullible heads that the specious claims of mass advertisements are mainly directed, as the recruiting posters and political slogans are aimed at Jimmy's.

Even the brief glimpse we have of Mr. Healey is a telling one. Sympathetic and considerate he may be, but Mr. Bryant is demoted just the same.

The settings for the play can be either elaborately built or quite simple. It would be a great pity if any company or society were to be frightened off attempting a production by the fact that there are three different scenes. With a certain amount of ingenuity from the scenic designer the sets can be erected and struck in a relatively small space, and the use of one or two small boat-trucks will help towards making the changes quick and smooth. The main object should be to make the rooms appear real, actual homes lived in by the intensely real characters who inhabit them. Act One is a real clutter of domestic and other articles so that one feels the rubbish of years has collected in the less accessible holes and corners. Act Two is much tidier, but still the main living-room of the house. Absence of children and more time to spare for housework are both evident. Act Three is neater still, a room rarely used though much decorated and polished for the party. One wonders, rather apprehensively, what sort of books the swivel bookcase contains!

Lighting is quite straightforward, with only a few simple cues in Act One. The general effect should be colder and greyer in Act Three than in the previous two.

A note on the Norfolk dialect is to be found on page 71.

Variety of pace and mood throughout is important. In several places—the meal in Act One for instance—it will be found that pieces of business have not many lines to cover them. This is quite deliberate, and the silences which fall are necessary and intentional; the action should not be hurried in order to fill them.

The play is an exciting and richly satisfying one to produce. It will repay all the care and attention which can be devoted to it and give an audience not only enjoyment and stimulation, but something to think about and to remember.

IVAN BUTLER

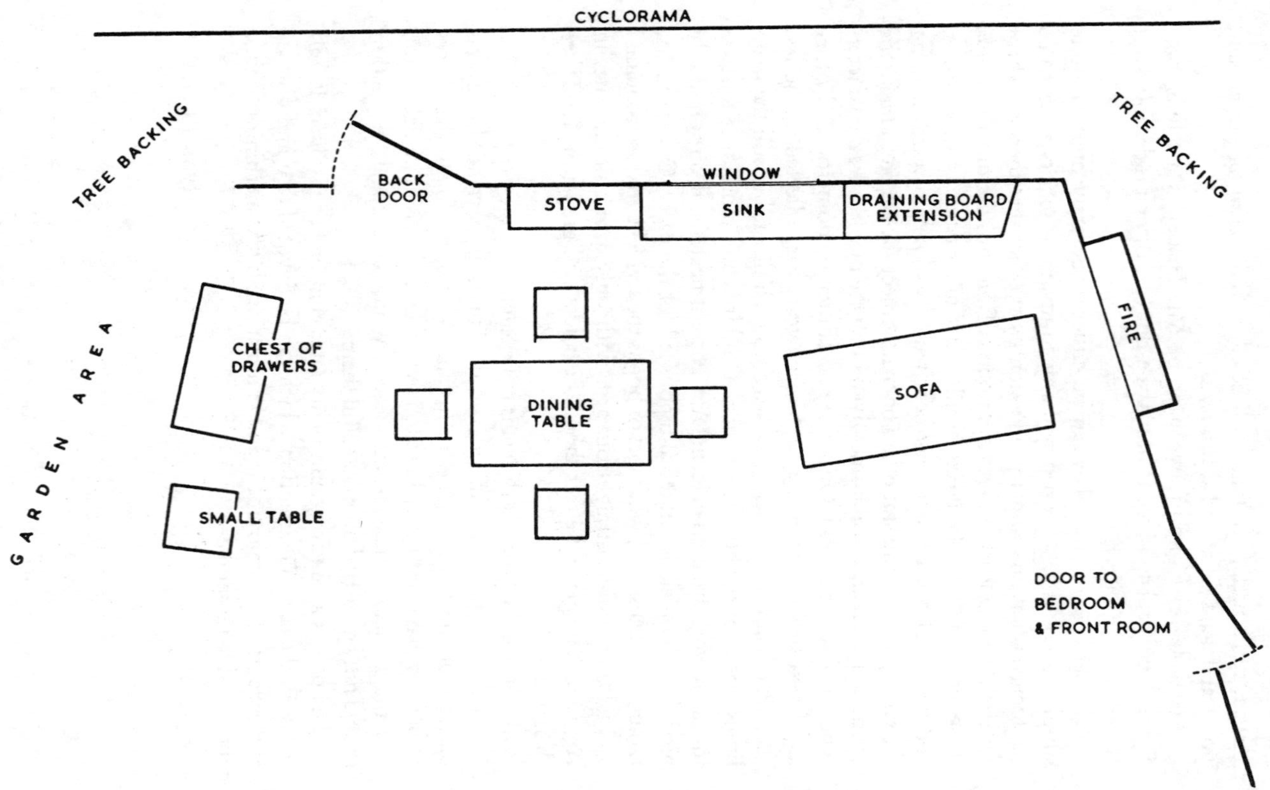
CYCLORAMA
TREE BACKING
TREE BACKING
BACK DOOR
WINDOW
STOVE
SINK
DRAINING BOARD EXTENSION
FIRE
CHEST OF DRAWERS
DINING TABLE
SOFA
SMALL TABLE
GARDEN AREA
DOOR TO BEDROOM & FRONT ROOM

ROOTS

ACT ONE

A rather ramshackled house in Norfolk where there is no water laid on nor electricity, nor gas. Everything rambles and the furniture is cheap and old. If it is untidy, it is because there is a child in the house and few amenities so that the mother is too overworked to take much care.

An assortment of clobber lies around: papers and washing, coats and basins, a tin wash tub with shirts and underwear to be cleaned, tilly lamps and primus stoves. Washing hangs on a line in the room. It is September.

> JENNY BEALES *is by the sink washing up. She is singing a recent pop song. She is short, fat, and friendly and wears glasses. A child's voice is heard from the bedroom off* L. *crying,* "Sweet, mamma, sweet". JENNY *crosses to stove to test potatoes.*

JENNY (*good naturedly*). Shut you up, Daphne, and get you to sleep now.
> (*Moves to get a dishcloth.*)

CHILD'S VOICE. Daphy wan sweet, sweet, sweet.

JENNY (*going to sideboard* R. *to get sweet*). My word, child, father come home and find you awake he'll be after you. (*Disappears off* L. *to bedroom with sweet.*) There—now sleep, gal; don't wan you grumpy wi' me in mornin'.

> (*Enter* JIMMY BEALES, U.R. *Also short, chubby, blond though hardly any hair left, ruddy complexion. He is a garage mechanic. Wears blue dungarees and an army pack slung over his shoulder. He wheels his bike in and lays it by the wall,* U.R. *Seems to be in some sort of pain—around his back.* JENNY *returns.*)

Waas matter wi' you then? (*Crosses to sideboard to replace sweets.*)

JIMMY. I don' know, gal. There's a pain in my guts and one a'tween my shoulder blades I can hardly stand up.

JENNY. Sit you down then an' I'll git you your supper on the table.

JIMMY (*to sofa,* U.L.). Blust gal! I can't eat yit.

> (JIMMY *picks up sofa pillow and lays down on the sofa—holding pillow to stomach.* JENNY *watches him a while.*)

JENNY (*up to cooker*). Don't you know what t'is yit? (*Strains potatoes.*)

JIMMY. Well, how should I know what t'is?

JENNY (*mashing potatoes*). I told Mother about the pain and she say it's indigestion.

JIMMY. What the hell's indigestion doin' a'tween my shoulder blades then?

JENNY. She say some people get indigestion so bad it go right through their stomach to the back.

JIMMY. Don't be daft.

JENNY. That's what I say. Blust Mother, I say, you don't git indigestion in the back. Don't you tell me, she say, I hed it! (*Stirs onions in frying pan on stove.*)

JIMMY. What hevn't she hed?

(JENNY *returns to washing up while* JIMMY *struggles awhile on the sofa.* JENNY *hums. No word. Then—*)

JENNY. Who d'you see today?

JIMMY. Only Doctor Gallagher.

JENNY (*wheeling round*). You see who?

JIMMY. Gallagher. His wife driv him up in the ole Armstrong.

JENNY (*taking two plates from oven*). Well I go t'hell if that ent a rum thing.

JIMMY (*rising and going to table. Pain has eased*). What's that then?

JENNY (*moving to get him supper from oven*). We was down at the whist drive in the village and that Judy Maitland say he were dead. Cos you know he've hed a cancer this last year and they don't give him no longer'n three weeks, don't you?

JIMMY. Ole crows. They don' wan' nothin' less than a death to wake them up.

JENNY. No. No longer'n three weeks.

GIRL'S VOICE (*off*). Yoo-hoo! Yoo-hoo!

JIMMY. There's your sister.

JENNY. That's her.

GIRL'S VOICE (*off*). Yoo-hoo! Any one home?

JENNY (*calling*). Come you on in, gal, don't you worry about yoo-hoo.

(*Enter* BEATIE BRYANT, U.R., *an ample, blonde, healthy-faced young woman of twenty-two years. She is carrying a case, which she puts down below sideboard,* R.C.)

JIMMY. Here she is. (*Sits at table.*)

JENNY (*with reserve, but pleased*).   Hello, Beatrice—how are you? (*Serving potatoes to* JIMMY.)

BEATIE (*with reserve, but pleased*). Hello, Jenny—how are you? What's that lovely smell I smell?

JENNY. Onions for supper and bread for the harvest festival.

BEATIE. Watcha Jimmy Beales, how you doin', bor?

JIMMY. Not so bad, gal, how's yourself?

BEATIE. All right you know. (*To below table and* L. *of it.*) When you comin' to London again for a football match?

JIMMY. O blust, gal, I don' wanna go to any more o' those things. Ole father Bryant was there in the middle of that crowd and he turn round an' he say (*Imitating.*) stop you a pushin' there, he say, stop you a pushin'.

JENNIE. Where's Ronnie? (*Serves her own plate.*)

BEATIE. He's comin' down at the end of two weeks. (*Takes off coat and puts it on sofa.*)

JIMMY. Ent you married yit?

BEATIE. No.

JIMMY. You wanna hurry then, gal, a long engagement don't do the ole legs any good.

JENNY. Now shut you up, Jimmy Beales, and get that food down you. Every time you talk, look, you miss a mouthful! That's why you complain of pain in your shoulder blades.

BEATIE. You bin hevin' pains then, Jimmy?

JIMMY. Blust yes! Right a'tween my shoulder blades.

JENNY. Mother says it's indigestion.

BEATIE. What the hell's indigestion doin' a'tween his shoulder blades?

JENNY. Mother reckon some people get indigestion so bad that go right through their stomach to the back.

BEATIE. Don't talk daft! (*Sits on sofa and glances at comic which she picks up from under cushion.*)

JENNY. That's what I say. Blust Mother, I say, you don' git indigestion in the back. Don't you tell me, she say, I hed it! (*Still busy serving.*)

BEATIE. What hevn't she hed? How is she?

JENNY. Still the same you know. How long you staying this time?

BEATIE. Two days here—two weeks at home.

JENNY. Hungry, gal? (*Back to stove.*)

BEATIE. Watcha got?

JENNY. Watcha see.

BEATIE. Liver? I'll hev it! (*She makes herself comfortable.*)
    (*Nearby are a pile of comics.* BEATIE *picks one up and reads.*)

JENNY (*dishing up* BEATIE'S *plate*). We got some ice cream after.

BEATIE (*absorbed*). Yerp.

JENNY. Look at her. No sooner she's in than she's at them ole comics. You still read them ole things?

JIMMY. She don't change much do she?

BEATIE. Funny that! Soon ever I'm home again I'm like I always was —it don' even seem I bin away. I do the same lazy things an' I talk the same. Funny that!

JENNY. What do Ronnie say to it?

BEATIE. He don't mind. He don't even know though. He ent never bin here. Not in the three years I known him. But I'll tell you, (*She jumps up and moves around as she talks.*) I used to read the comics he bought for his nephews and he used to get riled.

> (*Now* BEATIE *begins to quote* RONNIE, *and when she does she imitates him so well in both manner and intonation that in fact, as the play progresses, we see a picture of him through her.*)

(*Crosses to sit at table, L. side.*) "Hell, woman, what can they give you that you can *be* so absorbed?" So you know what I used to do? I used to get a copy of the "Manchester Guardian" and sit with that wide open—and a comic behind!

JIMMY. "Manchester Guardian"? Blimey Joe—he don' believe in hevin' much fun then?

BEATIE. That's what I used to tell him. "Fun?" he say, "fun? Playing an instrument is fun, painting is fun, reading a book is fun, talking with friends is fun—but a comic? A comic? For a young woman of twenty-two?"

JENNY (*handing out meal and sitting down herself*). He sound a queer bor to me. You eat, gal.

BEATIE (*enthusiastically*). He's alive though.

JIMMY. Alive? Alive you say? What's alive about someone who can't read a comic? What's alive about a person that reads books and looks at paintings and listens to classical music?

> (*There is a silence at this, as though the question answers itself— reluctantly:*
> JENNY *fetches ice cream for* JIMMY.)

JIMMY. Well, it's all right for some, I suppose.

BEATIE. And then he'd sneak the comic away from me and read it his-self!

JENNY (*giving* JIMMY *his ice-cream*). Oh, he didn't really mind then? (*Sits and continues eating.*)

BEATIE. No—'cos sometimes I read books as well. "There's nothing wrong with comics," he'd cry—he stand up on a chair when he want to preach but don't wanna sound too dramatic.

JIMMY. Eh?

BEATIE. Like this look. (*Stands on her chair.*) "There's nothing wrong with comics only there's something wrong with comics all the time. There's nothing wrong with football, only there's something wrong with only football. There's nothing wrong with rock'n rolling, only God preserve me from the girl that can do nothing else!" (*She half sits down and then stands up again, remembering something else.*) Oh, yes "and there's nothing wrong with talking about the weather, only don't talk to me about it!" (*Sits down.*)

(JIMMY *and* JENNY *look at each other as though she, and no doubt Ronnie, is a little barmy.* JIMMY *rises and gets coat from sofa and gaiters from mantel.*)

JENNY. He never really row with you then?

BEATIE. We used to. There was a time when he handled all official things for me you know. Once I was in between jobs and I didn't think to ask for my unemployment benefit. He told me to. But when I asked they told me I was short on stamps and so I wasn't entitled to benefit. I didn't know what to say but he did. He went up and argued for me—he's just like his mother, she argue with everyone—and I got it. I didn't know how to talk see, it was all foreign to me. Think of it! An English girl born and bred and I couldn't talk the language—except for to buy food and clothes. And so sometimes when he were in a black mood he'd start on me. "What can you talk of?" he'd ask. "Go on, pick a subject. Talk. Use the language. Do you know what language is?" Well, I'd never thought before—hev you?—it's automatic to you—isn't it? —like walking. "Well, language is words" he'd say, as though he were telling me a secret. "It's bridges, so that you can get safely from one place to another. And the more bridges you know about the more places you can see!" (*To* JIMMY.) And do you know what happens when you can see a place but you don't know where the bridge is?

JIMMY (*angrily*). Blust gal, what the hell are you on about? (*Sits on chair below table to fasten gaiters.*)

BEATIE. Exactly! You see, you hev a row! Still, rows is all right. I like a row. So then he'd say: "Bridges! Bridges! Bridges! Use your bridges, woman. It took thousands of years to build them, use them!" And that riled me. "Blust your bridges," I'd say. "Blust you and your bridges—I want a row." Then he'd grin at me. "You want a row?" he'd ask. "No bridges this time?" "No bridges," I'd say—and we'd row. Sometimes he hurt me but then, slowly, he'd built the bridge up for me—and then we'd make love! (*Innocently finishing her meal.*)

JENNY. You'd what, did you say?

>   (JENNY *rises, collects* JIMMY'S *and* BEATIE'S *plates and crosses up to sink for three sweets.*)

BEATIE. Make love. Love in the afternoon, gal. Ever had it? It's the only time for it. Go out or entertain in the evenings; sleep at night, study, work and chores in the mornings but love—alert and fresh, when you got most energy—love in the afternoon.

JIMMY. I suppose you take time off from work every afternoon to do it?

BEATIE. I'm talking about weekends and holidays—daft.

JENNY. Oh, Beatie, go on wi' you!

BEATIE. Well, go t'hell, Jenny Beales, you're blushin'. Ent you never had love in the afternoon? Ask Jimmy then.

JENNY (*returning with sweets*). Shut you up gal and get on wi' your ice-cream. It's strawberry flavour. (*Sits* R. *of table.*) Wan't some more vanilla, James?

JIMMY (*taking it in the middle of lacing up boots*). Yes, please. (*Eating.*) Good cream, ent it? Made from the white milk of a Jersey cow.

BEATIE. This is good, too—made from pink milk, ent it?

>   (*Pause.*)

JIMMY. Yerp! (*Pause.*) Come from a pink cow!

>   (*Pause. They are all enjoying the cream.*)

JENNY (*eating*). You remember Dickie Smart, Beatie?

BEATIE (*eating*). Who?

JENNY (*eating*). We hed a drink wi' him in the Storks when you was down last.

BEATIE (*eating*). Yerp.

JENNY (*eating*). Well, he got gored by a bull last Thursday. His left ear was nearly off, his knee were gored, his ribs bruised and the ligament of his legs torn.

>   (*Pause as they finish eating.*)

BEATIE (*euphemistically*). He hed a rough time then!
JENNY. Yerp. (*To* JIMMY *who has risen.*) You off now?
JIMMY. Mm.

> (JIMMY *crosses* U.R. *for reap hook and then to sideboard for sharpening stone.* JENNY *collects dishes and moves up to sink.*)

BEATIE. Still got your allotment, Jimmy?
JIMMY (*resuming his seat*). Yerp.
BEATIE. Bit heavy going this weather.
JIMMY. That ent too bad just yit—few more weeks an' the old mowld'll cling.
BEATIE. Watcha got this year?
JIMMY (*starts to sharpen reap hook*). Hed spuds, carrots, cabbages, you know. Beetroot, lettuces, onions, and peas. But me runners let me down this year though.
JENNY. I don't go much on them old things.
BEATIE. You got a fair owle turn then?
JIMMY. Yerp.
BEATIE (*jumping up*). I'll help you wash.
JENNY. That's all right, gal.
BEATIE. Where's the cloth?
JENNY. Here t'is.

> (BEATIE *helps collect dishes from table and proceeds to help wash up. This is a silence that needs organizing. Throughout the play there is no sign of intense living from any of the characters—*BEATIE'*s bursts are the exception. They continue in a routine rural manner. The day comes, one sleeps at night, there is always the winter, the spring, the autumn and the summer—little amazes them. They talk in fits and starts mainly as a sort of gossip and they talk quickly, too, enacting as though for an audience what they say. Their sense of humour is keen and dry. They show no affection for each other—though this does not mean they would not be upset were one of them to die. The silences are important—as important as the way they speak if we are to know them.*)

JENNY. What about that strike in London? Whaas London like wi'out the buses?
BEATIE. Lovely! No noise—and the streets, you should see the streets, flowing with people—the city looks human.
JIMMY. They wanna call us territorials out—we'd soon break the strike.
BEATIE. That's a soft thing for a worker to say for his mates.

JIMMY. Soft be buggered, soft you say? What they earnin' those bus-
men, what they earnin'? And what's the farm workers' wage? Do
you know it, gal?

BEATIE (*to sideboard with cutlery*). Well, let the farm workers go on
strike too then! It don't help a farm labourer if a busman don't go
on strike, do it now?

JENNY. You know they've got a rise though. Father Bryant's go up
by six and six a week as a pigman and Frank goes up seven'n six a
week for driving a tractor.

JIMMY. But you watch the Hall sack some on 'em.

JENNY. Thaas true, Beatie. They're such cods, honest to God they are.
Every time there's bin a rise someone get sacked. Without fail. You
watch it—you ask Father Bryant when you get home, ask him who's
bin sacked since the rise.

BEATIE. One person they 'ont sack is him though. They 'ont find
many men'd tend to pigs seven days a week and stay up the hours
he do.

JENNY. Bloody fool! (*Pause.*) Did Jimmy tell you he've bin chosen
for the Territorials' Jubilee in London this year?

BEATIE. What's this then? What'll you do there?

JIMMY. Demonstrate and parade wi' arms and such like.

BEATIE. Won't do you any good.

JIMMY. Don't you reckon? Gotta show we can defend the country,
you know. Demonstrate arms and you prevent war.

BEATIE (*she has finished putting cutlery away*). Won't demonstrate anything, bor. (*Goes to undo her case.*) Present for the house! (*Gives
present to* JENNY *who crosses with it to* L. *of table.*) Have a hydrogen
bomb fall on you and you'll find them things silly in your hands.
(*Searches for other parcels.*)

JIMMY. So you say, gal? So you say? That'll frighten them other
bastards though.

BEATIE. Frighten yourself y'mean. (*Finds parcels.*) Presents for the
kid. (*Crosses to* R. *of table.*)

JIMMY. And what do you know about this all of a sudden?

JENNY (*revealing a tablecloth*). Thank you very much, Beatie. Just what
I need.

BEATIE. You're not interested in defending your country, Jimmy, you
just enjoy playing soldiers.

JIMMY. What did I do in the last war then—sing in the trenches?

BEATIE. Ever heard of Chaucer, Jimmy?

JIMMY. No.

BEATIE (*sitting on* D.R. *end of table*). Do you know the M.P. for this constituency?

JIMMY. What are you drivin' at, gal—don't give me no riddles.

BEATIE. Do you know how the British Trade Union Movement started? And do you believe in strike action?

JIMMY. No to both those.

BEATIE. What you goin' to war to defend then?

JIMMY (*he is annoyed now*). Beatie—you bin away from us a long time now—you got a boy who's educated an that and he's taught you a lot maybe. (*To sideboard with sharpening stone.*) But don't you come pushin' ideas across at us—we're all right as we are. You can come when you like an' welcome but don't bring no discussion of politics in the house wi' you 'cos that'll only cause trouble. I'm telling you.

(*He goes off* U.R.)

JENNY. Blust gal, if you hevn't touched him on a sore spot. He live for them territorials he do—that's half his life.

BEATIE (*she is upset now*). What's he afraid of talking for?

JENNY. He ent afraid of talking, Beatie—blust he can do that gal.

BEATIE. But not talk, not really talk, not use bridges. I sit with Ronnie and his friends sometimes and I listen to them talk about things and you know I've never heard half of the words before.

JENNY (*crossing to sideboard with presents and wrapping.*) Don't he tell you what they mean?

BEATIE (*sitting chair* R. *of table*). I get annoyed when he keep tellin' me —and he want me to ask. (*Imitates him half-heartedly now.*) "Always ask, people love to tell you what they know, always ask and people will respect you."

JENNY. And do you?

BEATIE. No! I don't! An' you know why? Because I'm stubborn, I'm like mother, I'm stubborn. Somehow I just can't bring myself to ask, and you know what? I go mad when I listen to them. As soon as they start to talk about things I don't know about or I can't understand I get mad. They sit there, casually talking, and suddenly they turn on you, abrupt. "Don't you think?" they say. Like at school, pick on you and ask a question you ent ready for. Sometimes I don't say anything, sometimes I go to bed or leave the room. Like Jimmy—just like Jimmy.

JENNY. And what do Ronnie say to that then?

R.–B

Act Three]

BEATIE. He get mad, too. "Why don't you ask me, woman, for God's sake, why don't you ask me? Aren't I dying to tell you about things? Only ask!"

JENNY. And he's goin' to marry you? (*Up to sink to tidy plates.*)

BEATIE. Why not?

JENNY. Well I'm sorry, gal, you mustn't mind me saying this, but it don't seem to me like you two got much in common.

BEATIE (*loudly*). It's not true! We're in love!

JENNY. Well, you know.

BEATIE (*softly*). No, I don't know. I won't know till he come here. From the first day I went to work as waitress in the Dell Hotel and saw him working in the kitchen I fell in love—and I thought it was easy. I thought everything was easy. I chased him for three months with compliments and presents until I finally give myself to him. He never said he love me nor I didn't care but once he had taken me he seemed to think he was responsible for me and I told him no different. I'd make him love me I thought. I didn't know much about him except he was different and used to write most of the time. And then he went back to London and I followed him there. (*Rising and crossing slowly* D.L.) I've never moved far from home but I did for him and he felt all the time he couldn't leave me and I didn't tell him no different. And then I got to know more about him. He was interested in all the things I never ever thought about. About politics and art and all that, and he tried to teach me. He's a socialist and he used to say you couldn't bring socialism to a country by making speeches, but perhaps you could pass it on to someone who was near you. So I pretended I was interested—but I didn't understand much. All the time he's trying to teach me but I can't take it, Jenny. And yet, at the same time, I want to show I'm willing. I'm not used to learning. Learning was at school and that's finished with.

JENNY (*moves to table and brushes off crumbs*). Blust gal, you don't seem like you're going to be happy then. Like I said.

BEATIE. But I love him.

JENNY. Then you're not right in the head then.

BEATIE. I couldn't have any other life now.

JENNY. Well I don't know and that's a fact.

BEATIE (*playfully mocking her*). Well I don't know and that's a fact! (*Suddenly.*) Come on, gal, I'll teach you how to bake some pastries. (*Crosses to case for apron.*)

JENNY. Pastries?

BEATIE. Ronnie taught me.

JENNY. Oh, you learnt that much then?

BEATIE. But he don't know. I always got annoyed when he tried to teach me to cook as well—Hell! I had to know something—but it sank in all the same.

> (*By this time it has become quite dark and* JENNY *proceeds to light a tilly lamp at the table.*)

JENNY. He use a sledge hammer for that?

BEATIE (*moving to* R. *of table*). Oh don't you worry, gal, it'll be all right once we're married. Once we're married and I got babies I won't need to be interested in half the things I got to be interested in now.

JENNY. No you won't, will you! Don't need no education for babies.

BEATIE. Nope. Babies is babies—you just have 'em.

JENNY. Little cods!

BEATIE. You gonna hev another, Jenny?

JENNY. Well, course I am. What you on about? Think Jimmy don't want none of his own?

BEATIE (*sitting* R. *of table*). He's a good man, Jenny.

JENNY. Yerp.

BEATIE. Not many men'd marry you after you had a baby.

JENNY (*pumping the lamp*). No.

BEATIE. He didn't ask you any questions? Who was the father? Nor nothing?

JENNY. No.

BEATIE. You hevn't told no one, hev you, Jenny?

JENNY. No, that I hevn't.

BEATIE. Well, that's it, gal, don't you tell me then!

> (JENNY *has finished pumping the tilly lamp and we are in brightness.*)

JENNY (*severely*). Now Beatie, stop it. Every time you come home you ask me that question and I hed enough. (*Crosses quickly to sink and continues to tidy up.*) It's finished with and over. No one don't say nothing and no one know. You hear me?

BEATIE (*rising and moving* D.L.). Are you in love with Jimmy?

JENNY. Love? I don't believe in any of that squit—we just got married, that's that.

BEATIE (*suddenly looking around the room at the general chaos*). Jenny Beales, just look at this house. Look at it!

JENNY. I'm looking. What's wrong?

BEATIE. Let's clean it up.

JENNY. Clean what up?

BEATIE. Are you going to live in this house all your life?

JENNY. You gonna buy us another?

BEATIE. Stuck out here in the wilds with only ole Stan Mann and his
missus as a neighbour and sand pits all around. Every time it rain
look you're stranded.

JENNY. Jimmy don't earn enough for much more'n we got.

BEATIE. But it's so dirty.

JENNY. You wait till you got a two year old kid.

BEATIE. Let's make some order—I love tidying up.

JENNY. What about the pastries? Pastries! Oh my sainted aunt, the
bread!

> (JENNY *dashes to the oven and brings out a most beautiful looking
> plaited loaf of bread.*)

(*Admiring it.*) Well, no one wanna complain after that. Isn't that
beautiful, Beatie?

BEATIE. I could eat it now.

JENNY. You hungry again?

BEATIE (*making an attack on the clothes that are lying around, folding them,
and putting them on the table*). I'm always hungry again. Ronnie say
I eat more'n I need. "If you get fat, woman, I'll leave you—without
even a discussion!"

JENNY (*placing bread on large oval plate to put away*). Well, there ent
nothin' wrong in bein' fat.

BEATIE. You ent got no choice, gal. (*Seeing bike standing* U.R.) A bike!
What's a bike doin' in a livin' room—I'm putting it outside.

JENNY. Jimmy 'ont know where it is.

BEATIE. Don't be daft, you can't miss a bike. (*Wheels it off* U.R. *and
calls from there.*) Jenny! Start puttin' the clothes away.

JENNY (*places bread on sideboard*). Blust gal, I ent got nowhere to put
them.

BEATIE (*from outside*). You got drawers—you got cupboards.

JENNY. They're full already.

BEATIE (*entering—energy sparks from her*). Come here—let's look.
(*Looks.*) Oh, go away—you got enough room for ten families. You
just bung it all in with no order, that's why. Here—help me.

> (*They drag out all manner of clothes from the drawers of the side-
> board and begin to fold them up at table.*)

BEATIE. How's my Frankie and Pearl?

JENNY. They're all right. You know she and Mother don't talk to each other?

BEATIE. What, again? Who's fault is it this time?

JENNY. Well, Mother she say it's Pearl's fault and Pearl she say it's Mother.

BEATIE. Well, they wanna get together quick and find whose fault it is 'cos I'm going to call the whole family together for tea to meet Ronnie.

JENNY. Well, Susan and Mother don't talk neither so you got a lot of peace making to do.

BEATIE. Well go t'hell, what's broken them two up?

JENNY. Susan hev never bin struck on her mother, you know that, don't you?—well, it seems that Susan bought something off the club from Pearl and Pearl give it to Mother and Mother sent it to Susan through the fishmonger what live next door her in the council houses. And of course Susan were riled 'cos she didn't want her neighbours to know that she bought anything off the club. So they don't speak.

BEATIE. Kids! It makes me mad.

JENNY. And you know what t'is with Pearl, don't you?—it's 'cos Mother hev never thought she was good enough for her son Frankie.

BEATIE. No more she wasn't neither!

JENNY. What's wrong wi' her then? I get on all right.

BEATIE. Nothing's wrong wi' her, she just wasn't good enough for our Frankie, that's all.

JENNY. Who's being small minded now?

BEATIE. Always wantin' more'n he can give her.

(BEATIE *stands on sofa, gets clothes from line and takes them to* table.)

JENNY. An' I know someone else who always wanted more'n she got.

BEATIE (*sulkily*). It's not the same thing.

JENNY. Oh yes t'is.

BEATIE. T'ent.

JENNY. T'is, my gal. (*Mimicking the child* BEATIE.) I wan a 'nana, a 'nana, a 'nana. Frankie's got my 'nana, 'nana, 'nana.

(*They move to sideboard and start putting clothes away in drawers.*)

BEATIE. Well, I liked bananas.

JENNY. You liked anything you could get your hands on and Mother used to give in to you 'cos you were the youngest. Me and Susan and Frankie never got nothing 'cos o' you—'cept a clout round the ear.

BEATIE. T'ent so likely. You got everything and I got nothing.

JENNY. All we got was what we pinched out the larder and then you used to go and tell tales to Mother.

BEATIE. I never did.

JENNY. Oh, didn't you, my gal? Many's the time I'd've willingly strangled you—with no prayers—there you are, no prayers whatsoever. Strangled you till you was dead.

BEATIE. Oh go on wi' you, Jenny Beales.

(*By now they have finished folding the clothes and have put away most of the laundry and garments that have till this moment cluttered up the room.* BEATIE *says "there", stands up and looks around, finds some coats sprawled helter skelter and hangs them up behind the door.*)

I'll buy you some coat hangers.

JENNY (*finishing at sideboard*). You get me a couple o' coats to hang on 'em first please.

BEATIE (*looking around*). What next? Bottles, jars, nicknacks, saucepans, cups, papers—everything anywhere. Look at it! Come on!

. (BEATIE *attempts to get these things into either their proper place or out of sight.*)

JENNY (*watching her*). You hit this place like a bloody whirlwind you do, like a bloody whirlwind. Jimmy'll think he've come into the wrong house and I shan't be able to find a thing.

BEATIE. Where's the broom? (*She finds it beside the stove and is now gurgling with sort of animal noises signifying excitement. Her joy is childlike.*) How's Poppy?

JENNY. Tight as ever.

BEATIE (*sweeping floor*). What won't he give you now?

JENNY. T'ent nothing wi' me gal. Nothing he do don't affect me. It's Mother I'm referring to.

BEATIE. Don't he still give her much money?

JENNY. Money? She hev to struggle and skint all the time—all the time. Well it ent never bin no different from when we was kids, hev it?

BEATIE. No.

(*During next speech* JENNY *takes milk bottles from sink off* U.R. *then returns to sink to put plates in rack.*)

JENNY. I tell you what. It wouldn't surprise me if Mother were in debt all the time, that it wouldn't. No. It wouldn't surprise me at all.

BEATIE. Oh, never.

JENNY (*moving above table*). Well, what do you say that for, Beatie—do you know how much he allow her a week look?

BEATIE. Six pounds?

JENNY. Six pound be buggered. Four pound ten! An' she hev to keep house an' buy her own clothes out of that.

BEATIE. Still, there's only two on 'em.

JENNY. You try keepin' two people in food for four pound ten. She pay seven an' six a week into Pearl's club for clothes, two and six she hev on the pools and a shilling a week on the Labour Tote. (*Suddenly.*) Blust! I forgot to say. Pearl won the Tote last week.

BEATIE. A hundred pounds?

JENNY. A hundred pounds! An' ole Mrs. Dyson what used to live Starston way, she come up second wi' five pounds and seventy.

BEATIE (*sweeping dust out of doors*). Well no one wrote me about it.

JENNY. Cos you never wrote no one else.

BEATIE. What she gonna do wi' it—buy a TV?

JENNY. TV? Blust no. You know she hevn't got electricity in that house. No, she say she's gonna get some clothes for the kids.

(*There is a sound now of a drunk old man approaching and alongside of it the voice of* JIMMY. *The drunk is singing:* "I come from Bungay Town, I calls I Bungay Johnnie." JENNY *crosses up to door.*)

Well I go t'hell if that ent Stan Mann drunk again. And is that Jimmy wi' him? (*Listens.*)

BEATIE (*replacing broom by stove*). But I thought Stan Mann was paralysed.

JENNY. That don't stop him getting paralytic drunk. (*Listens again.*) That's Jimmy taking him into the house I bet. A fortune that man hev drunk away—a whole bleedin' fortune. (*Moves back to sink.*) Remember the fleet of cars he used to run and all that land he owned, and all them cattle he had and them fowl? Well, he've only got a few acres left and a few ole chickens. He drink it all away. Two strokes he've had from drinking and now he's paralysed down one side. But that don't stop him getting drunk—no it don't.

(JIMMY *enters and throws his jacket on chair* R. *of table, sits below table and takes off his boots and gaiters and grunts meanwhile.*)

JIMMY. Silly ole bastard.

JENNY. I was just telling Beatie how he've drunk a fortune away, hevn't he?

JIMMY. He wanna drink a little more often and he'll be finished for good.

JENNY. Didn't he hev all them cows and cars and land, Jimmy? And didn't he drink it all away bit by bit?

JIMMY. Silly ole cod don't know when to stop.

JENNY. I wished I had half that money he drink.

JIMMY. He messed his pants.

JENNY. He what? Well where was this then?

JIMMY. By the allotment.

JENNY. Well, what did you do then?

(*During the following speech* JIMMY *takes his gaiters to mantel and then crosses to place his boots by the sink.*)

JIMMY. He come up to me—'course I knowed he were drunk the way he walk—he come up to me an' he say, "Even Jimmy Beales, thaas a fine turnover you got there". An' I say, yerp t'is. An' then he bend down to pick a carrot from the ground an' then he cry, "oops, I done it again"! An' 'course, soon ever he say "done it again" I knowd what'd happen. So I took his trousers down and ran the ole hose over him.

BEATIE (*moving to* R. *of sofa*). Oh, Jimmy, you never did.

JIMMY. I did gal. I put the ole hose over him and brought him home along the fields with an ole sack around his waist.

BEATIE. He'll catch his death.

JIMMY. Never—he's strong as an ox.

JENNY. What'd you do with his trousers and things?

JIMMY (*going up to door*). Put it on the compost heap—good for the land!

(*Now* STAN MANN *enters* U.R. *and stands inside doorway. He's not all that drunk. The cold water has sobered him a little. He is old—about sixty-five—and despite his slight stoop one can see he was a very strong upright man. He probably looks like every man's idea of a farmer —except that he wears no socks or boots at this moment and he hobbles on a stick.*)

STAN. Sorry about that, ole son.

JIMMY. Don't you go worrying about that, my manny—get you along to bed.

JENNY. Get some shoes on you too, Stan, or you'll die of cold and booze.

STAN (*screwing up his eyes*). Is that you, Jenny? Hello ole gal. How are you?

JENNY. It's you you wanna worry about now, ole matey. I'm well enough.

STAN (*screwing up his eyes still more*). Who's that next to you?

JENNY. Don't you recognize her? It's our Beatie, Stan.

STAN (*crossing and sitting R. end of sofa*). Is that you, Beatie? Well blust gal, you gotten fatter since I seen you last. You gonna be fat as Jenny here? Come on over an' let's look at you.

BEATIE (*sits sofa L. of STAN*). Hello Stan Mann, how are you?

STAN (*looking her up and down*). Well enough, gal, well enough. You married yit?

BEATIE. No.

STAN. You bin courtin' three years. Why ent you married yit?

BEATIE (*slightly embarrassed*). We ent sure yit.

STAN. You ent sure, you say? What ent you sure of? You know how to do it, don't you?

JENNY (*moving to sofa*). Go on wi' you to bed, Stann Mann.

STAN. Tell your boy he don't wanna waste too much time or I'll be hevin' yer myself for breakfast—on a plate.

JENNY. Stan Mann, I'm sendin' you to your bed—go on now, (*Lifting him and taking him U.R.*) off wi' you, you can see Beatie in the mornin'.

STAN (*as he is ushered out—to BEATIE*). She's fat, ent she? I'm not sayin' she won't do mind, but she's fat. (*As he goes out with JENNY.*) All right ole sweetheart, I'm goin', I'm just right for bed. Did you see the new bridge they're building? It's a rum ole thing isn't it . . . (*Out of sound.*)

JIMMY (*sitting R. of table*). Well, I'm ready for bed.

BEATIE. I can't bear sick men. They smell.

JIMMY. Ole Stan's all right—do anythin' for you.

BEATIE. I couldn't look after one you know.

JIMMY. Case of hevin' to sometimes.

BEATIE. Ronnie's father's paralysed like that. I can't touch him.

JIMMY. Who see to him then?

BEATIE. His mother. She wash him, change him, feed him. Ronnie help sometimes. I couldn't though. Ronnie say, "Christ woman, I hope you aren't around when I'm ill." (*Shudders.*) Ole age terrify me.

JIMMY. Where you sleepin' tonight, gal?

BEATIE. On the couch in the front room, I suppose.

JIMMY. You comfortable sleepin' on that ole thing? You wanna sleep with Jenny while you're here?

BEATIE. No thanks, Jimmy. (*She is quite subdued now.*) I'm all right on there.

JIMMY. Right, then I'm off. (*Rising and looking around.*) Where's the "Evening News" I brought in.

JENNY (*entering U.R.*). You off to bed?

JIMMY. Yerp. Reckon I've had 'nough of this ole day. Where's my News?

JENNY. Where d'you put it, Beatie?

JIMMY (*moving above table and suddenly seeing the room*). Blust, you movin' out?

BEATIE. Here you are, Jimmy Beales. (*Hands him paper from sofa.*) It's all tidy now.

JIMMY. So I see. Won't last long though, will it? Night. (*Goes off L. to bed.*)

JENNY. Well I'm ready for my bed, too—how about you Beatie?

BEATIE (*rising*). Yerp.

JENNY (*taking a candle in a stick and lighting it*). Here, take this with you. Your bed's made. Want a drink before you turn in?

BEATIE. No thanks, gal.

JENNY (*picking up tilly lamp and making towards L. door*). Right then. Sleep well, gal.

BEATIE (*going after JENNY with candle*). Good night, Jenny. (*She pauses half-way. Loud whispers from now on.*) Hey, Jenny.

JENNY (*turning*). What is it?

BEATIE. I'll bake you some pastries when I get to Mother's.

JENNY. Father won't let you use his electricity for me, don't talk daft.

BEATIE. I'll get Mother on to him, it'll be all right. Your ole ovens weren't big 'nough anyways. Good night.

JENNY. Good night.

BEATIE (*an afterthought*). Hey, Jenny.

JENNY. What now?

BEATIE. Did I tell you I took up painting?

JENNY. Painting?

BEATIE. Yes—on cardboard and canvases with brushes.

JENNY. What kind of painting?

BEATIE. Abstract painting—designs and patterns and such like. I can't do nothing else. I sent two on 'em home. Show you when you come round—if Mother hevn't thrown them out.

JENNY. You're an artist then?

BEATIE. Yes. Good night.

JENNY. Good night. (*She goes off.*)

> BEATIE *slowly follows* JENNY *off leaving the room in darkness.*
> *Perhaps we see only the faint glow of moonlight from outside and then*

THE CURTAIN FALLS.

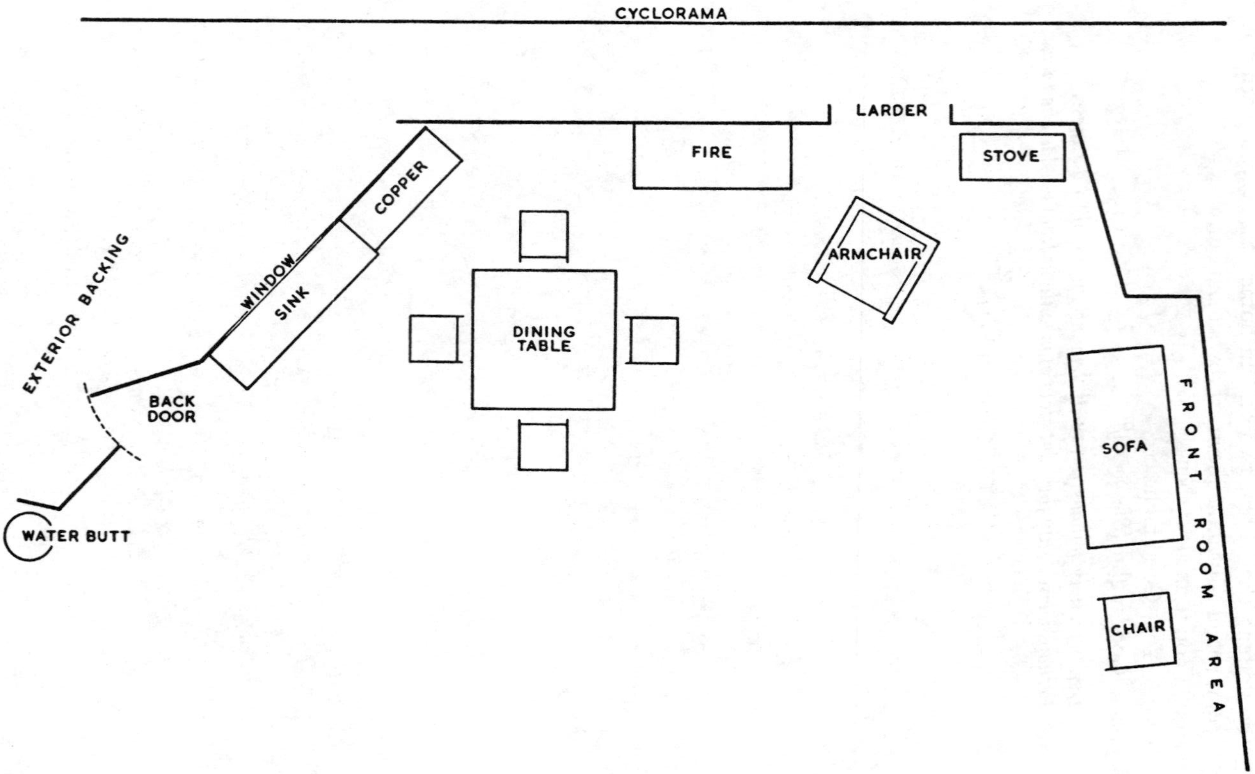
CYCLORAMA
LARDER
FIRE
STOVE
COPPER
WINDOW
SINK
EXTERIOR BACKING
ARMCHAIR
DINING TABLE
BACK DOOR
WATER BUTT
SOFA
FRONT ROOM AREA
CHAIR

ACT TWO

Scene 1

Two days have passed. BEATIE will arrive at her own home, the home of her parents. This is a tied cottage on a main road between two large villages. It is neat and ordinary inside. We can see a large kitchen—where most of the living is done—and attached to which is a large larder U.L.; also part of the front room L. and a piece of the garden where some washing is hanging R.

> MRS. BRYANT *is a short, stout woman of fifty. She spends most of the day on her own and consequently when she has a chance to speak to anybody she says as much as she can as fast as she can. The only people she sees are the tradesmen, her husband, the family when they pop in occasionally. She speaks very loudly all the time so that her friendliest tone sounds aggressive, and she manages to dramatize the smallest piece of gossip into something significant. Each piece of gossip is a little act done with little looking at the person to whom it is addressed. At the moment she is at the door R. leading to the garden looking for the cat.*

MRS. BRYANT. Cossie, Cossie, Cossie! Cossie, Cossie, Cossie! Here Cossie! Food Cossie! Cossie, Cossie, Cossie! Blust you, cat, where the hell are you? Oh hell on you then, I ent wastin' my time wi' you now.

> *(She returns to the kitchen and thence to larder from which she emerges with some potatoes. These she starts peeling at the sink. STAN MANN appears round the back door R. He has a handkerchief to his nose and is blowing vigorously, as vigorously as his paralysis will allow. MRS. BRYANT looks up but continues her peeling.)*

STAN *(crossing and sitting L. of table)*. Rum thing to git a cold in summer, what you say, Daphne?

MRS. BRYANT. What'd you have me say, my manny? Sit you down, bor, and rest a bit. Shouldn't wear such daf' clothes.

STAN. Daf' clothes? Blust woman! I got on half a cow's hide, what you sayin'! Where's the gal?

MRS. BRYANT. Beatie? She 'ent come yit. Didn't you see her?

STAN. Hell, I was up too early for her. She always stay the week-end wi' Jenny 'fore commin' home?

MRS. BRYANT. Most times.

(STAN *sneezes.*)

What you doin' up this way wi' a cold like that then? Get you home to bed.

STAN. Just come this way to look at the vicarage. Stuff's comin' up for sale soon.

MRS. BRYANT. You still visit them things then?

STAN. Yerp. Pass the ole time away. Pass the ole time.

MRS. BRYANT. Time drag heavy then?

STAN. Yerp. Time drag heavy. She do that. Time drag so slow, I get to thinkin' it's Monday when it's still Sunday. Still, I had my day, gal, I say. Yerp. I had that all right.

MRS. BRYANT. Yerp. You had that an' a bit more, ole son. I shan't grumble if I last long as you.

STAN. Yerp. I hed my day. An' I'd do it all the same again, you know that? Do it all the same I would.

MRS. BRYANT. Blust! All your drinkin' an' that?

STAN.. Hell! Thaas what kep' me goin' look. Almost anyways. None o' them young 'uns'll do it, hell if they will. There ent much life in the young 'uns. Bunch o' weak kneed ruffians. None on 'em like livin' look, none on 'em! You read in them ole papers what go on look, an' you wonder if they can see. You do! Wonder if they got eyes to look around them. Think they know where they live? Corse they don't, they don't you know, not one. Blust! the winter go an' the spring come on after an' they don't see buds an' they don't smell no breeze an' they don't see gals, an' when they see gals they don't know whata do wi' 'em. They don't!

MRS. BRYANT. Oh hell, they know that all right.

STAN. Gimme my young days an' I'd show 'em. Public demonstrations I'd give!

MRS. BRYANT (*placing potatoes on stove*). O shut up, Stan Mann.

STAN. Just gimme young days again, Daphne Bryant, an' I'd take you. But they 'ont come again, will they gal?

MRS. BRYANT. That they 'ont.

STAN. No, they 'ont that! Rum ole thing the years, ent they? (*Pause.*) Them young 'uns is all right though. Long as they don't let no one fool them, long as they think it out theirselves. (*Sneezes and coughs.*)

MRS. BRYANT (*moving to help him up*). Now get you back home Stan
Mann. (*Good naturedly.*) Blust, I aren't hevin' no dead 'uns on me
look. Take a rum, bor, take a rum an' a drop o' hot milk and get to
bed. What's Mrs. Mann thinking of lettin' you out like this?

> (*She pulls the coat round the old man and pushes him off* R. *He
> goes off mumbling.*)

STAN. She's a good gal, she's right 'nough, she don't think I got it
this bad. I'll pull this ole scarf round me. Hed this scarf a long
time, hed it since I started wi' me cars. She bought it me. Lasted a
long time. Shouldn't need it this weather though. (*He has gone.*)

MRS. BRYANT (*mumbling same time as* STAN *and moving* U.R. *to sink*).
Go on, off you go. Silly ole bastard, runnin' round with a cold like
that. Don't know what 'es doin' half the time. Poor ole man.
Cossie? Cossie? That you, Cossie? (*Looks through into the front room
and out of window at* STAN.) Poor ole man.

> (*After peeling some seconds she turns the radio on, turning the dial
> knob through all manner of stations and back again until she finds some
> very loud dance music which she leaves blaring on. Audible to us, but
> not to* MRS. BRYANT *is the call of* "Yoo-hoo, Mother, yoo-hoo".
> BEATIE *appears round the garden and peers into the kitchen.* MRS.
> BRYANT *jumps.*)

Blust, you made me jump.

BEATIE (*enters and tones radio down*). Can't you hear it? Hello, Mother.
(*Kisses her.*)

MRS. BRYANT. Well, you've arrived then.

BEATIE. Didn't you get my card?

MRS. BRYANT. Came this morning.

BEATIE (*placing her case on table*). Then you knew I'd arrive.

MRS. BRYANT. Course I did.

BEATIE. My things come?

MRS. BRYANT. One suitcase, one parcel in brown paper—

BEATIE. My paintings.

MRS. BRYANT. And one other case.

BEATIE. My pick up. D'you see it?

MRS. BRYANT. I hevn't touched a thing.

BEATIE. Bought myself a pick-up on the H.P.

MRS. BRYANT. Don't you go telling that to Pearl.

BEATIE. Why not?

MRS. BRYANT. She'll wanna know why you didn't buy off her on the club.

BEATIE. Well, hell, Mother, I weren't gonna hev an ole pick up sent me from up north somewhere when we lived next door to a gramophone shop.

MRS. BRYANT. No. Well, what bus you come on—the half past ten one?

BEATIE. Yerp. Picked it up on the ole bridge near Jenny's.

MRS. BRYANT. Well I looked for you on the half past nine bus and you weren't on that so I thought to myself I bet she come on the half past ten and you did. You see ole Stan Mann?

BEATIE. Was that him just going up the road?

MRS. BRYANT. Wearin' an ole brown scarf, that was him.

BEATIE. I see him! Just as I were comin' off the bus. Blust! Jimmy Beale's give him a real dowsin' down on his allotment 'cause he had an accident.

MRS. BRYANT. What, another?

BEATIE. Yerp.

MRS. BRYANT. Poor ole man. Thaas what give him that cold then. He come in here sneezin' fit to knock hisself down.

BEATIE. Poor ole bastard. Got any tea, Ma? I'm gonna unpack.

(BEATIE *goes into front room with case. We see her take out frocks which she puts on hangers, and underwear and blouses which she puts on couch.*)

MRS. BRYANT. Did you see my flowers as you come in? Got some of my hollyhocks still flowering. Creeping up the wall they are— did you catch a glimpse on 'em? And my asters and geraniums? Poor ole Joe Simonds gimme those afore he died. Lovely geraniums they are.

BEATIE. Yerp.

MRS. BRYANT. When's Ronnie coming?

BEATIE. Saturday week—an' Mother, I'm heving all the family along to meet him when he arrive so you patch your rows wi' them.

MRS. BRYANT. What you on about, gal? What rows wi' them?

BEATIE. You know full well what rows I mean—them ones you hev wi' Pearl and Susan.

MRS. BRYANT. T'ent so likely. They hev a row wi' me, gal, but I give 'em no heed, that I don't. (*Hears van pass on road.*) There go Sam Martin's fish van. He'll be calling along here in an hour.

BEATIE (*entering with very smart dress and coming below table*). Like it, Mother?

MRS. BRYANT. Blust gal, that's a goodun, ent it! (*She moves* R.C. *to look.*) Where d'you buy that then?

BEATIE (*holding dress against her*). Swan and Edgars.

MRS. BRYANT. Did Ronnie choose it?

BEATIE. Yerp.

MRS. BRYANT (*sitting R. of table*). He've got good taste then.

BEATIE. Yerp. Now listen, Mother, I don't want any on you to let me down. When Ronnie come I want him to see we're proper. I'll buy you another bowl so's you don't wash up in the same one as you wash your hands in and I'll get some more tea-cloths so's you don't use the towels. And no swearin'.

MRS. BRYANT. Don't he swear then?

BEATIE. He swear all right, only I don't want him to hear you swear.

MRS. BRYANT. Hev you given it up then?

BEATIE. Mother, I've never swore.

MRS. BRYANT. Go to hell, listen to her!

BEATIE (*sitting in chair above table*). I never did, now! Mother, I'm telling you, listen to me. Ronnie's the best thing I've ever had and I've tried hard for three years to keep hold of him. I don't care what you do when he's gone but don't show me up when he's here.

MRS. BRYANT. Speak to your Father, gal.

BEATIE. Father, too. I don't want Ronnie to think I come from a small minded family. "I can't bear mean people" he say. "I don't care about their education, I don't care about their past as long as their minds are large and inquisitive, as long as they're generous."

MRS. BRYANT. Who say that?

BEATIE. Ronnie.

MRS. BRYANT. He talk like that?

BEATIE. Yerp.

MRS. BRYANT. Sounds like a preacher.

BEATIE (*standing on the chair*). "I don't care if you call me a preacher, I've got something to say and I'm going to say it. I don't care if you don't like being told things—we've come to a time when you've got to say this is right and this is wrong. God in heaven, have we got to be wet all the time? Well, have we?" Hell, Mother, you've got them ole wasps still flying around. (*She waves her arms in the air flaying the wasps.*) September and you've still got wasps. Owee! Shoo-shoo! (*In the voice of her childhood.*) Mammy, Mammy, take them ole things away. I doesn't like them—ooh! Nasty things.

> (BEATIE *jumps off chair and picks up coat hanger from table. Now both she and her mother move stealthily around the room hunting wasps. Occasionally* MRS. BRYANT *strikes one dead or* BEATIE *spears*

one against the wall. MRS. BRYANT *conducts herself matter of fact like but* BEATIE *makes a fiendish game of it.*)

MRS. BRYANT. They're after them apples on that tree outside. (*Moving down to door.*) Go on! Off we' you! Outside now! There—that's got 'em out, but I bet the bastards'll be back in a jiffy look.

BEATIE. Oh yes, an' I want to have a bath.

MRS. BRYANT. When d'you want that then?

BEATIE. This morning.

MRS. BRYANT. You can't heve no bath this morning, that copper won't heat up till after lunch.

BEATIE. Then I'll bake the pastries for Jenny this morning and you can put me water on now. (*She returns to table* R. *to place dress on hanger.*)

MRS. BRYANT. I'll do that now then. I'll get you the soft water from the tank.

> (MRS. BRYANT *now proceeds to collect bucket and move back and forth between the garden out of view and the copper in the kitchen. She fills the copper with about three buckets of water and then lights the fire underneath it. In between buckets she chats.*)

(*Off*—*as she hears lorry go by.*) There go Danny Oakley to market. (*She returns with first bucket.*)

BEATIE. Mother! I dreamt I died last night and heaven were at the bottom of a pond. You had to jump in and sink and you know how afeared I am of water. It was full of film stars and soldiers and there were two rooms. In one room they was playing skiffle and—and— I can't remember what were goin' on in the other. Now who was God? I can't remember. It was someone we knew, a she. (*Returns to front room to unpack.*)

MRS. BRYANT (*entering with second bucket. Automatically*). Yerp. (*Pause.*) You hear what happened to the headache doctor's patient? You know what they say about him—if you've got a headache you're all right but if you've got something more you've had it! Well he told a woman not to worry about a lump she complained of under her breast and you know what that were? That turned out to be thrombosis! There! Thrombosis! She had that breast off. Yes, she did. Had to hev it cut off. (*Goes for next bucket.*)

BEATIE (*automatically*). Yerp. (*She appears from front room with two framed paintings. She sets them up and admires them. They are primitive —red, black and yellow—see Dusty Bicker's work.*) Mother! Did I write and tell you I've took up painting? I started five months ago. Working in gouache. Ronnie says I'm good. Says I should carry on and maybe I can sell them for curtain designs. "Paint, girl" he say. "Paint! The world is full of people who don't do the things they want so you paint and give us all hope!"

(MRS. BRYANT *enters*.)

BEATIE (*showing the paintings*). Like 'em?

MRS. BRYANT (*looks at them a second*). Good colours, ent chey? (*She is unmoved and continues to empty third bucket while* BEATIE *returns paintings to other room.*) Yes gal, I ent got no row wi' Pearl but I ask her to change my Labour Tote man 'cos I wanted to give the commission to Charlie Gorleston and she didn't do it. Well, if she can be like that I can be like that, too. You gonna do some baking you say?

BEATIE (*enters from front room putting on pinafore and carrying a parcel*). Right now. Here y'are, Daphne Bryant, present for you. I want eggs, flour, sugar and marg. I'm gonna bake a sponge and give it frilling. (*Goes to larder to collect things.*)

MRS. BRYANT (*unpacking parcel* R. *of table. It is a pinafore*). We both got one now.

(MRS. BRYANT *returns to sink to continue to peel potatoes as* BEATIE *at table proceeds to separate four eggs, the yolk of which she starts whipping with sugar. She sings meanwhile a ringing folk song.*)

BEATIE. Oh a dialogue I'll sing you as true as me life
    Between a coal owner and poor pitman's wife.
    As she were a walking along the highway
    She met a coal owner and to him did say,
        "Derry down, down, down Derry down."
    Whip the eggs till they're light yellow he says.

MRS. BRYANT. Who says?

BEATIE. Ronnie.
    "Good morning, Lord Firedamp," the good woman said,
    "I'll do you no harm, sir, so don't be afraid.
    If you'd been where I'd been for most of my life
    You wouldn't turn pale at a poor pitman's wife."
        Singing down, down, down Derry down.

MRS. BRYANT. What song's that?

BEATIE. A coalmining song.

MRS. BRYANT. I tell you what I reckon's a good song, that "I'll wait for you in the heaven's blue". I reckon that's a lovely song, I do. Jimmy Samson he sing that.

BEATIE. It's like twenty other songs, it don't mean anything and·it's sloshy and sickly.

MRS. BRYANT. Yes, I reckon that's a good song that.

BEATIE (*suddenly crossing to* MRS. BRYANT). Listen, Mother, let me see if I can explain something to you. Ronnie always say that's the point of knowing people. "It's no good having friends who scratch each other's back," he say. "The excitement in knowing people is to hand on what you know and to learn what you don't know. Learn from me" he say, "I don't know much but learn what I know." So let me try and explain to you what he explain to me.

MRS. BRYANT (*on hearing a bus*). There go the half past eleven bus to Diss—blust that's early. (*Puts potatoes in saucepan on oven and goes to collect runner beans which she prepares.*)

BEATIE (*following her around*). Mother, I'm talking to you. Blust, woman, it's not often we get together and really talk, it's nearly always me listening to you telling who's dead. Just listen a second.

MRS. BRYANT (*back at sink*). Well go on, gal, but you always take so long to say it.

BEATIE (U.R. *of table*). What are the words of that song?

MRS. BRYANT. I don't know all the words.

BEATIE. I'll tell you.

(*Recites them.*)

I'll wait for you in the heaven's blue
As my arms are waiting now.
Please come to me and I'll be true
My love shall not turn sour.
I hunger, I hunger, I cannot wait longer,
My love shall not turn sour.

There! Now what do that mean?

MRS. BRYANT (*surprised*). Well, don't you know what that mean?

BEATIE (*moving to her mother again*). I mean what do they do to you? How do the words affect you? Are you moved? Do you find them beautiful?

MRS. BRYANT. Them's as good words as any.

BEATIE. But do they make you feel better?

MRS. BRYANT. Blust gal! Them ent supposed to be a laxative!

BEATIE. I must be mad to talk with you.

MRS. BRYANT. Besides it's the tune I like. Words never mean anything.

BEATIE. All right, the tune then! What does that do to you? Make your belly go gooey, your heart throb, makes your head spin with passion? Yes, passion, Mother, know what it is? Because you won't find passion in that third rate song, no you won't!

MRS. BRYANT (*salting the vegetables she has prepared*). Well all right, gal, so it's third rate you say. Can you say why? What make that third rate and them frilly bits of opera and concert first rate? 'sides, did I write that song? Beatie Bryant, you do go up and down in your spirits and I don't know what's gotten into you, gal, no I don't.

BEATIE. I don't know either, Mother. I'm worried about Ronnie, I suppose. I have that same row with him. I ask him exactly the same questions—what make a pop song third rate. And he answer and I don't know what he talk about. (*Sitting above table.*) Something about registers, something about commercial world blunting our responses. "Give yourself time, woman" he say. "Time! You can't learn how to live overnight. I don't even know" he say, "and half the world don't know but we got to try. Try" he say, "cos we're still suffering from the shock of two world wars and we don't know it. Talk" he say, "and look and listen and think and ask questions." But Jesus! I don't know what questions to ask or how to talk. And he gets so riled—and yet sometimes so nice. "It's all going up in flames" he say, "but I'm going to make bloody sure I save someone from the fire."

MRS. BRYANT (*moves to and fro from stove with saucepans*). Well I'm sure I don't know what he's on about. Turn to your baking, gal, look and get you done, Father'll be home for his lunch in an hour.

(*A faint sound of an ambulance is heard.* MRS. BRYANT *looks up but says nothing.* BEATIE *turns to whipping the eggs again and* MRS. BRYANT *to cleaning the runner beans. Out of this pause* MRS. BRYANT *begins to sing* "I'll wait for you in heaven's blue's", *but on the second line she hums the tune incorrectly.*)

BEATIE (*laughs*). No, no, hell Mother, it don't go like that. It's—

(BEATIE *corrects her and in helping her mother she ends by singing the song, with some enthusiasm, to the end. For tune see page 70.*)

MRS. BRYANT (*smiling across at* BEATIE). Thank God you come home sometimes, gal—you do bring a little life with you anyway.

BEATIE. Mother, I ent never heard you express a feeling like that.

MRS. BRYANT (*she is embarrassed and pushes* BEATIE L. *in order to lay table*). The world don't want no feelings, gal. (*Footsteps are heard.*) Is that your father home already?

(MR. BRYANT *appears at the door and lays a bicycle against the wall. He is a small shrivelled man wearing denims, a peaked cap, boots and gaiters. He appears to be in some pain.*)

BEATIE (*moving down* L. *of table*). Hello, Poppy Bryant.

MR. BRYANT. Hello Beatie. You're here then.

MRS. BRYANT. What are you home so early for?

MR. BRYANT. The ole guts ache again. (*Sits in armchair* U.L. *and grimaces.*)

MRS. BRYANT. Well, what is it?

MR. BRYANT. Blust woman, I don't know what t'is n'more'n you, do I?

MRS. BRYANT. Go to the doctor, man, I keep telling you.

BEATIE (*sitting* R. *of table*). What is it, Father Bryant?

MRS. BRYANT. He got gut's ache.

BEATIE. But what's it from?

MR. BRYANT. I've just said I don't know.

MRS. BRYANT. Get you to a doctor, man, don't be so soft. You don't want to be kept from work, do you?

MR. BRYANT. That I don't, no I don't. Hell, I just see ole Stan Mann picked up an' thaas upset me enough.

MRS. BRYANT. Picked up you say?

MR. BRYANT. Well, didn't you hear the ambulance?

MRS. BRYANT. There! I hear it but I didn't say narthin'. Was that for Stan Mann then?

MR. BRYANT. I was cyclin' along wi' Jack Stones and we see this here figure on the side o' the road there an' I say, "thaas a rum shape in the road, Jack", and he say, "blust that's ole Stan Mann from Heybrid," an't'were. 'Corse soon every he see what t'were, he rushed off for 'n'ambulance and I waited alongside Stan.

BEATIE. But he just left here.

MRS. BRYANT. I see it comin'. He come in here an' I shoved him off home. Get you to bed and take some rum an' a drop o' hot milk, I tell him.

BEATIE. Is he gonna die?

MR. BRYANT. Wouldn't surprise me, that it wouldn't. Blust, he look done in.

MRS. BRYANT (*crosses to sink for plates*). Poor ole fellah. Shame though, ent it?

MR. BRYANT. When d'you arrive, Beatie?

MRS. BRYANT. She come in the half past ten bus. I looked for her on the nine-thirty bus and she weren't on that so I thought to myself I bet she come on the half past ten. She did.

MR. BRYANT. Yerp.

MRS. BRYANT (*moving to stove for plates for warming*). You gonna stay away all day?

MR. BRYANT. No I aren't. I gotta go back 'cos one of the ole sows is piggin'. Spect she'll be hevin' them in a couple of hours. (*To* BEATIE.) Got a sow had a litter o' twenty-two. (*Picks up paper to read.*)

BEATIE (*rises and crosses to sink with eggs*). Twenty-two? Oh pop, can I come see this afternoon.

MR. BRYANT. Yerp.

MRS. BRYANT (*wiping down stove*). Thought you was hevin' a bath.

BEATIE. Oh yes. I forgot. I'll come tomorrow then.

MR. BRYANT. They'll be there. What you doin', gal?

MRS. BRYANT. She's baking a sponge, now leave her be.

MR. BRYANT. Oh, you learnt something in London then.

BEATIE. Ronnie taught me.

MR. BRYANT. Well where is Ronnie then?

MRS. BRYANT. He's comin' on Saturday a week an' the family's goin' to be here to greet him.

MR. BRYANT. All on 'em?

BEATIE.
MRS. BRYANT. } All on 'em!

MR. BRYANT. Well that'll be a rum gatherin' then.

MRS. BRYANT. And we've to be on our best behaviour.

MR. BRYANT. No cussin' and swearin'?

MRS. BRYANT.
BEATIE. } No.

MR. BRYANT. Blust, I shan't talk then.

(*A young man,* MR. HEALEY, *appears round the garden—he is the farmer's son and manager of the estate* BRYANT *works for.*)

MRS. BRYANT (*seeing him first*). Oh, Mr. Healey, yes. Jack! It's Mr. Healey. Do come in, sir.

(MR. BRYANT *rises and moves to* C. *and* HEALEY *enters and joins
him.* HEALEY *speaks in a firm, not unkind, but business-is-business
voice. There is that apologetic threat even in his politeness.*)

MR. HEALEY. You were taken ill.

MR. BRYANT. It's all right, sir, only gut's ache, won't be long goin'.
The pigs is all seen to, just waiting for the ole sow to start.

MR. HEALEY. What time you expecting it?

MR. BRYANT. Oh, she 'ont come afore two this afternoon, no she 'ont
be much afore that.

MR. HEALEY. You're sure you're well, Jack? I've been thinking that
it's too much for you carting those pails round the yard.

MR. BRYANT. No, that ent too heavy, sir, 'course 't'ent. You don't
wanna worry, I'll be along after lunch. Just an ole gut's ache, that's
all—seein' the doctor tonight—eat too fast probably.

MR. HEALEY. If you're sure you're all right, then I'll put young Daniels
off. You can manage without him now we've fixed the new pump in.

MR. BRYANT. I can manage sir—'course I can.

MR. HEALEY (*moving off outside*). All right then, Jack. I'll be with you
around two o'clock. I want to take the old one out of number three
and stick her with the others in seventeen. The little ones won't need
her, will they? Then we'll have them sorted out tomorrow.

MR. BRYANT (*moving with him*). That's right, sir, they can go on their
own now, they can, I'll see to it tomorrow.

MR. HEALEY. Right then, Jack. (*Pausing in doorway.*) Oh—you hear
Stan Mann died?

MR. BRYANT. He died already? But I saw him off in the ambulance
no more'n half hour ago.

MR. HEALEY. Died on the way to hospital. Jack Stones told me. Lived
in Heybrid, didn't he?

MR. BRYANT. Alongside my daughter.

MR. HEALEY (*going and calling*). Well, good morning, Mrs. Bryant.

MRS. BRYANT (*calling*). Good morning, Mr. Healey.

(*The two men nod to each other,* MR. HEALEY *goes off.* MR.
BRYANT *lingers a second.*)

MRS. BRYANT (*to* BEATIE). That was Mr. Healey, the new young
manager.

BEATIE. I know it, Mother.

MR. BRYANT (*returning slowly to his armchair*). He's dead then.

MRS. BRYANT. Who? Not Stan Mann.

MR. BRYANT. Young Healey just tell me.

MRS. BRYANT (*finishes setting table and sits above it*). Well I go t'hell. An' he were just here look, just here along side ' me not more'n hour past.

MR. BRYANT. Rum, ent it?

BEATIE (*weakly*). Oh hell, I hate dying.

MRS. BRYANT. He were a good ole bor though. Yes, he was. A good ole stick. There!

BEATIE (*sitting R. of table*). Used to ride me round on his horse, always full o' life an' jokes. "Tell your boy he wanna hurry up and marry you" he say to me "or I'll hev you meself, on a plate."

MRS. BRYANT. He were a one for smut though.

BEATIE. I was talkin' with him last night. Only last night he was tellin' me how he caught me pinchin' some gooseberries off his patch an' how he gimme a whole apron full and I went into one o' his fields near by an' ate the lot. "Blust" he say, "you had the ole guts ache", and' he laugh, sat there laughin' away to hisself.

MRS. BRYANT. I can remember that. Hell, Jenny'll miss him—used always to pop in an' out o' there's.

BEATIE. Seem like the whole world gone suddenly dead, don' it?

MR. BRYANT. Rum ent it?

(*Silence. MRS. BRYANT rises and crosses to larder for mustard which she makes at the sink.*)

MRS. BRYANT. You say young Healey tell you that? He's a nice man Mr. Healey is, yes he is, a good sort, I like him.

BEATIE. Sound like he were threatening to sack Father; don't know about being nice.

MR. BRYANT. That's what I say, get a rise and they start cutting down the men or the overtime.

MRS. BRYANT. The Union Magazine's come.

MR. BRYANT. I don't want that ole thing.

BEATIE (*rising and crossing to larder*). Why can't you do something to stop the sackings?

MR. BRYANT. You can't, you can't—that's what I say, you can't. Sharp as a pig's scream they are—you just can't do nothin'.

BEATIE. Mother, where's the bakin' tin?

MR. BRYANT. When we gonna eat that?

BEATIE. You ent! It's for Jenny Beales.

MR. BRYANT. You aren't making that for Jenny, are you?

BEATIE. I promised her.

MR. BRYANT. Not with my electricity, you aren't.

BEATIE (*moving above table*). But I promised, Poppy.

MR. BRYANT. That's no matters. I aren't spendin' money on electricity
 bills so's you can make every Tom Dick'n Harry a sponge cake,
 that I aren't.

MRS. BRYANT. Well, don't be so soft man, it won't take more'n half
 hour's bakin'.

MR. BRYANT. I don't care what it'll take, I say, I aren't lettin' her.
 Jenny wants cakes she can make 'em herself. So put that away,
 Beatie, and use it for something else.

MRS. BRYANT. You wanna watch what you're sayin' of 'cos I live
 here, too.

MR. BRYANT. I know all about that but I pay the electricity bill and
 I says she isn't bakin'.

BEATIE. But Poppy, one cake.

MR. BRYANT. No I say.

BEATIE (*crossing to sink*). Well, Mummy, do something—how can he
 be so mean?

MRS. BRYANT (*across to armchair*). Blust me if you ent the meanest ole
 cod that walks this earth. Your own daughter and you won't let
 her use your oven. You bloody ole hypercrite.

MR. BRYANT. You pay the bills and then you call names.

MRS. BRYANT. What I ever seen in you God only know. Yes! an'
 he never warn me. Bloody ole hypercrite!

MR. BRYANT. You pay the bills and then you call names I say.

MRS. BRYANT. On four pound ten a week? You want me to keep you
 and pay bills? Four pound ten he give me. God knows what he do
 wi' the rest. I don't know how much he've got. I don't, no I don't.
 Bloody ole hypercrite.

MR. BRYANT. Let's hev grub and not so much o' the lip woman.

   (BEATIE *begins to put the things away. She is on the verge of the
tears she will soon let fall.*)

MRS. BRYANT. That's how he talks to me—when he do talk. Cos you
 know he don't ever talk more'n he hev to, and when he do say
 something it's either "how much this cost?" or "lend us couple o'
 bob." He've got the money but sooner than break into that he
 borrow off me. Bloody ole miser. (*To* BEATIE *as she moves into the
 front room.*) What you canna cry for, gal? T' ent worth it. Blust,
 you don't wanna let an ole hypercrite like him upset you, no you

don't. I'll get my back on you, my manny, see if I don't. You won't get away with no tricks on me.

(BEATIE *returns with a small packet.*)

BEATIE (*throwing parcel in father's lap*). Present for you.

MRS. BRYANT. I'd give him presents that I would! I'd walk out and disown him! Beatie, now stop you a cryin' gal—blust, he ent worth cryin' for, that he ent. Stop it I say and we'll have lunch.

CURTAIN

SCENE 2

Lunch has been eaten. MR. BRYANT *is sitting above the table rolling himself a cigarette.* MRS. BRYANT *is collecting the dishes and taking them to a sink to wash up.* BEATIE *is taking things off the table and putting them into the larder—jars of sauce, plates of sliced bread and cakes, butter, sugar, condiments and bowl of tinned fruit.*

MRS. BRYANT (*to* BEATIE). Ask him what he want for his tea.

MR. BRYANT. She don't ever ask me before, what she wanna ask me now for?

MRS. BRYANT. Tell him it's his stomach I'm thinking about—I don't want him complaining to me about the food I cook.

MR. BRYANT. Tell her it's no matters to me—I ent got no pain now besides.

BEATIE. Mother, is that water ready for my bath?

MRS. BRYANT. Where you hevin' it?

BEATIE. In the kitchen of course.

MRS. BRYANT. Blust gal, you can't bath in this kitchen during the day. What if someone call at the door?

BEATIE. Put up the curtain then, I shan't be no more'n ten minutes.

MR. BRYANT. Sides, who want to see her in a dickey suit?

BEATIE (*standing beside him*). I know men as 'ould pay to see me in my dickey suit. (*Posing her plump outline.*) Don't you think I got a nice dickey suit?

(MR. BRYANT *makes a dive and pinches her bottom.*)

Ow! Stoppit Bryants, stoppit!

(*He persists.*)

Daddy, stop it now!

MRS. BRYANT. Tell him he can go as soon as he like, I want your bath over and done with.

BEATIE. Oh Mother, stop this nonsense do. If you want to tell him something tell him—not me.

MRS. BRYANT. I don't want to speak to him, hell if I do.

BEATIE. Father, get the bath in for me please. Mother, where's them curtains?

(MR. BRYANT *goes off to fetch a long tin bath—wide at one end, narrow at the other—while* MRS. BRYANT *leaves washing up to fish out some curtains which she hangs from one wall to another* U.R. *concealing thus a corner of the kitchen. Anything that is in the way is removed.* BEATIE *meanwhile brings out from the front room a change of underwear, the new frock, some soap, powder and towel. These she lays within each reach of the curtain.*)

BEATIE. I'm gonna wear my new dress and go across the fields to see Frankie and Pearl.

MRS. BRYANT. Frankie won't be there, what you on about? He'll be gettin' the harvest in.

BEATIE. You makin' anything for the harvest festival?

MR. BRYANT (*entering with bath, places behind curtain*). Your mother don't ever do anything for the harvest festival—don't you know that by now?

BEATIE. Get you to work father Bryant, I'm gonna plunge in water and I'll make a splash.

MRS. BRYANT. Tell him we've got kippers for tea and if he don't want none let him say now.

BEATIE. She says it's kippers for tea.

MR. BRYANT. Tell her I'll eat kippers. (*He goes, collecting bike on the way.*)

BEATIE. He says he'll eat kippers. Right now, Mother, you get cold water an' I'll pour the hot.

(*Each now picks up a bucket.* MRS. BRYANT *goes off out to collect the cold water and* BEATIE *plunges bucket into boiler to retrieve hot water. The bath is prepared with much child-like glee.* BEATIE *loves her creature comforts and does with unabashed, almost animal, enthusiasm that which she enjoys. When the bath is prepared,* BEATIE *slips behind the curtain to undress and enter.* MRS. BRYANT *goes off for more cold water.*)

MRS. BRYANT (*off*). You hear about Jimmy Skelton? They say he've bin arrested for approaching some man in the village.

BEATIE. Jimmy Skelton what own the pub?

MRS. BRYANT. That's him. I know all about Jimmy Skelton though. He were a young boy when I were a young girl. I always partner him at whist drives. He's been to law before, you know. Yes! An' he won the day, too! Won the day he did. I don't take notice, though, him and me gets on all right. What do Ronnie's mother do with her time?

BEATIE. She's got a sick husband to look after.

MRS. BRYANT (*enters and takes water up to alcove*). She an educated woman?

BEATIE. Educated? No. She's a foreigner. Nor ent Ronnie educated neither. He's an intellectual, failed all his exams. They read and things.

MRS. BRYANT. Oh, they don't do nothing then?

BEATIE. Do nothing? I'll tell you what Ronnie do, he work till all hours in a hot ole kitchen. An' he teach kids in a club to act and jive and such. And he don't stop at weekends either 'cos then there's political meetings and such and I get breathless trying to keep up wi' him. Ooohh, Mother it's hot.

MRS. BRYANT. I'll get you some more cold then.

BEATIE. No—ooh—it's lovely. The water's so soft Mother.

MRS. BRYANT. Yerp.

BEATIE. It's so soft and smooth. I'm in.

MRS. BRYANT. Don't you stay in too long, gal. There go the twenty minutes past one bus.

BEATIE. Oh Mother, me bath cubes. I forgot me bath cubes. In the little case by me pick up.

(MRS. BRYANT *goes into front room and returns with bath cubes.*)
(*Long pause.*)

Mother, these bath cubes smell beautiful. I could stay here all day.

MRS. BRYANT (*continuing her work*). I shall never forget when I furse heard on it. I was in the village and I was talking to Reggie Fowler. I say to him, there've bin a lot o' talk about Jimmy, ent there? Disgustin', I say. Still, there's somebody wanna make some easy money, you'd expect that in a village, wouldn't you? Yes, I say to

him, a lot of talk. An' he stood there, an' he were a lookin' at me
an' a lookin' as I were a talkin' and then he say, Misses, he say,
I were one o' the victims! Well, you could've hit me over the head
wi' a hammer. I was one o' the victims, he say. An' he tell me
afterwards, blust gal, you looked surprised. An' that I were, too.
Still, Jimmy's a good fellow with it all—do anything for you. I
partner him at whist drives; he bin had up scores o' times though.

BEATIE. Mother, what we gonna make Ronnie when he come?

MRS. BRYANT. Well, what do he like?

BEATIE. He like trifle and he like steak and kidney pie.

MRS. BRYANT. We'll make that then. So long as he don't complain o'
the gut's ache. Frankie hev it too sometimes and Jenny's husband James.

BEATIE. Know why? You all eat too much. The Londoners think
we live a healthy life but they don't know we stuff ourselves silly
till our guts ache. Look at that lunch we had. Lamb chops, spuds,
runner beans and three Yorkshire puddings.

MRS. BRYANT. But you know what's wrong wi' Jimmy Beales? It's
indigestion. He eat too fast.

BEATIE. What the hell's indigestion doin' a'tween his shoulder blades?

MRS. BRYANT. Cos some people get so bad it go right through their
stomach to the back.

BEATIE. You don't get indigestion in the back, Mother, what you on
about!

MRS. BRYANT. Don't you tell me, gal, I had it!

BEATIE. Owee! The soap's in me eyes—Mother, towel, the towel,
quickly the towel!

(MRS. BRYANT *hands in towel to* BEATIE. *The washing up is
probably done by now so* MRS. BRYANT *sits in the armchair, legs apart
and arms folded, thinking what else to say.*)

MRS. BRYANT. You heard that Ma Buckey hev been taken to mental
hospital in Norwich? Poor ole dear. If there's one thing I can't
abide that's mental cases. They frighten me—they do. Can't face
'em. I'd sooner follow a man to a churchyard than the mental
hospital. That's a terrible thing to see a person lose their reason—
that 't'is. Well, I tell you what, down where I used to live, down the
other side of the Hall, years ago we moved in next to an old woman.
I only had Jenny and Frank then—an' this woman she were the
sweetest of people. We used to talk and do errands for each other—
O she was a sweet ole dear. And then one afternoon I was going out

to get my washin' in and I saw her. She was standin' in a tub o' water up to her neck. She was! Up to her neck. An' her eyes had that glazed, wonderin' look and she stared straight at me she did. Straight at me. Well, do you know what? I was struck dumb. I was struck dumb wi' shock. What wi her bein' so nice all this while, the sudden comin' on her like that in the tub fair upset me. It did! And people tell me afterwards that she's bin goin' in an' out o'· hospital for years. Blust, that scare me. That scare me so much she nearly took me round the bend wi' her.

(BEATIE *appears from behind the curtain in her dressing gown and a towel round her head.*)

BEATIE.   There! I'm gonna hev a bath every day when I'm married.

(BEATIE *starts rubbing her hair with a towel and fiddles with radio. She finds a programme playing the slow movement from Mendelssohn's Fourth Symphony.* MRS. BRYANT *rises and unhitches curtains, folds them up and then they both lift up the bath and take it off into the garden. When they return* MRS. BRYANT *replaces the displaced furniture while* BEATIE *rubs her hair and stands before the mirror.*)

(*Looking at her reflection.*) Isn't your nose a funny thing, and your ears. And your arms and your legs, aren't they funny things— sticking out of a lump.

MRS. BRYANT (*switching off radio*). Turn that squit off!

BEATIE (*turning on her mother violently*). Mother! I could kill you when you do that. No wonder I don't know anything about any- thing. You give me nothing that was worthwhile, nothing. I never knowed anything about the news because you always switched off after the headlines. I never read any good books 'cos there was never any in the house. I never heard nothing but dance music because you always turned off the classics. I can't even speak English proper because you never talked about anything important.

MRS. BRYANT. What's gotten into you now, gal?

BEATIE (*up to window*). God in heaven, Mother, you live in the country but you got no—no—no majesty. You spend your time among green fields, you grow flowers and you breathe fresh air and you got no majesty. You go on and you go on talking and talking so your mind's cluttered up with nothing and you shut out the world. What kind of a life did you give me?

MRS. BRYANT (*busy at larder*). Blust gal, I weren't no teacher.

BEATIE. But you hindered. You didn't open one door for me. Even his mother cared more for me than what you did. Beatie, she say, Beatie, why don't you take up evening classes and learn something other than waitressing? Yes, she say, you won't ever regret learnin' things. But did you care what job I took up or whether I learned things? You didn't even think it was necessary.

MRS. BRYANT. I fed you. I clothed you. I took you out to the sea. What more d'you want? We're only country folk, you know. We ent got no big things here you know.

BEATIE (*slumping angrily into armchair*). Squit! Squit! It makes no difference country or town. All the town girls I ever worked with were just like me. It makes no difference country or town—that's squit. Do you know when I used to work at the holiday camp and I sat down with the other girls to write a letter we used to sit and discuss what we wrote about. An' we all agreed, all on us, that we started: "just a few lines to let you know" and then we get on to the weather and then we get stuck so we write about each other and after a page an' half of big scrawl end up "hoping this finds you as well as it leaves me". There! We couldn't say any more. Thousands of things happening at this holiday camp and we couldn't find words for them. All of us the same. Hundreds of girls and one day we're gonna be mothers and you still talk to me of Jimmy Skelton and the ole woman in the tub. Do you know I've heard that story a dozen times. A dozen times. Don't you know what you're talking about? Jesus, how can I bring Ronnie to this house.

MRS. BRYANT. Blust gal, if Ronnie don't like us then he—

BEATIE. Oh, he'll like you all right. He like most people. He'd've loved ole Stan Mann. Ole Stann Mann would've understood every-thing Ronnie talk about. Blust! That man liked livin'. Besides, Ronnie say it's too late for the old 'uns to learn. But he says it's up to us young 'uns. And them of us that know hev got to take them of us as don't know and bloody well teach them.

MRS. BRYANT. I bet he hev a hard job changing you, gal!

BEATIE. He's not trying to change me, Mother. You can't change people, he say, you can only give them some love and hope they'll take it. And that's what he's tryin' to do with me and I'm tryin' to understand—do you see that, Mother?

MRS. BRYANT. I don't see what that's got to do with music though.

BEATIE. Oh my God! (*Suddenly.*) I'll show you. (*Goes off to front room to collect pick-up and a record.*) Now sit you down in the armchair, gal, and I'll show you. Don't start ironing or reading or nothing just sit there and be prepared to learn something. (*Appears with pick-up and record.*) You aren't too old, just you sit and listen.

(MRS. BRYANT, *dazed by* BEATIE'S *attack, sits in armchair and watches her daughter preparing the equipment.*)

That's the trouble you see, we ent ever prepared to learn anything, we close our minds the minute anything unfamiliar appear. I could never listen to music. I used to like some on it but then I'd lose patience, I'd go to bed in the middle of a symphony, or my mind would wander 'cos the music didn't mean anything to me so I'd go to bed or start talking. "God almighty," he'd say, "don't you know something's happening around you? Aren't you aware of something that's bigger'n you? Sit back woman" he'd say, "listen to it. Let it happen to you and you'll grow as big as the music itself."

MRS. BRYANT. Blust he talk like a book.

BEATIE. An' sometimes he talk as though you didn't know where the moon or the stars was. (BEATIE *puts on record of the last movement of Bizet's L'arlésienne Suite.*) Now listen. This is a simple piece of music, it's not highbrow but it's full of living. You want to dance to it. And that's what he say socialism is. "Christ" he say "socialism isn't talking all the time, it's living, it's singing, it's dancing, it's being interested in what go on around you, it's being concerned about people and the world." Listen, Mother. (*She becomes breathless and excited.*) Listen to it. It's simple, isn't it? Can you call that squit?

MRS. BRYANT. I don't say it's all squit.

BEATIE. You don't have to frown because it's alive.

MRS. BRYANT. No, not all on it's squit.

BEATIE. See the way the other tune comes in? Hear it? Two simple tunes, one after the other.

MRS. BRYANT. I aren't saying it's all squit.

BEATIE. And now listen, listen, it goes together, the two tunes together, they knit, they're perfect. Don't it make you want to dance?

(*She begins to dance a mixture of a cossack dance and a sailor's hornpipe. The music becomes fast and her spirits are young and high.*)

Listen to that, Mother. Is it difficult? Is it squit? It's light. It make me feel light and confident and happy. God Mother, we could all be so much more alive and happy. Wheeeee.

BEATIE *claps her hands and dances on and her* MOTHER *smiles and claps her hands as*

THE CURTAIN FALLS.

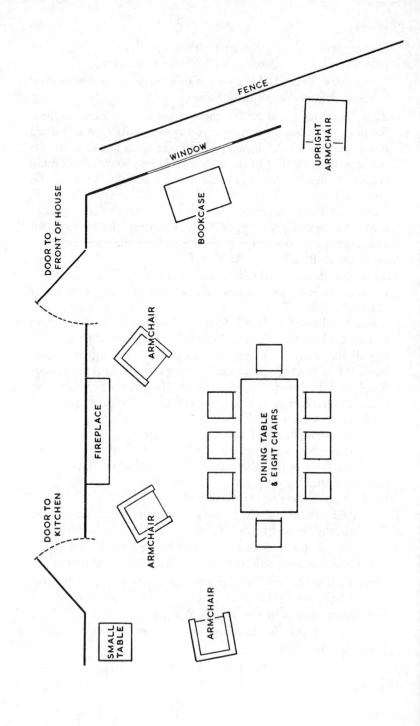

ACT THREE

Two weeks have passed. It is Saturday, the day Ronnie is to arrive. One of the walls of the kitchen is now pushed aside and the front room is revealed. It is low ceilinged, and has dark brown wooden beams. The furniture is not typical country farmhouse type. There may be one or two windsor-type straight back chairs but for the rest it is cheap utility stuff. Two armchairs, a table, a small bamboo table, wooden chairs, a small sofa and a swivel bookcase. There are a lot of flowers around—in pots on the window ledge and in vases on the bamboo table and swivel case.

 It is three in the afternoon, the weather is cloudy—it has been raining and is likely to start again. On the table is a spread of food (none of this will be eaten). There are cakes and biscuits on plates and glass stands. Bread and butter, butter in a dish, tomatoes, cheese, jars of pickled onions, sausage rolls, dishes of tinned fruit—it is a spread! Round the table are eight chairs. BEATIE's paintings are hanging on the wall. The room is empty because BEATIE is upstairs changing and MRS. BRYANT is in the kitchen. BEATIE—until she descends—conducts all her conversation shouting from upstairs.

BEATIE (*off*). Mother! What are you on at now?

MRS BRYANT (*from kitchen*). I'm just puttin' these *glass* cherries on the trifle.

BEATIE. Well come on, look he'll be here at four-thirty.

MRS. BRYANT (*from kitchen*). Don't you fret, gal, it's another hour'n half yet, the postman heven't gone by. (*Enters* U.R. *with a large bowl of trifle.*) There! He like trifle you say?

BEATIE. He love it.

MRS. BRYANT. Well he need to 'cos there's plenty on it. (*To herself, surveying the table.*) Yes there is, there's plenty on it. (*It starts to rain.*) Blust, listen to that weather.

BEATIE. Rainin' again!

MRS. BRYANT (*looking out of window*). Raining? It's rainin' fit to drowned you. (*Sound of bus.*) There go the three o'clock.

BEATIE. Mother, get you changed, come on, I want us ready in time.

MRS. BRYANT. Blust, you'd think it were the bloody Prince of Egypt comin'. (*Goes off* U.L. *upstairs.*)

 (*The stage is empty again for a few seconds. People are heard*

taking off their macs and exclaiming at the weather from the kitchen
U.R. *Enter* FRANK *and* PEARL BRYANT. *He is pleasant and dressed
in a blue pin-striped suit, is ruddy faced and blond haired. An odd sort
of shyness makes him treat everything as a joke. His wife is a pretty
brunette, young and simply dressed in a plain, flowered frock.*)

FRANK (*calling*). Well, where are you all? Come on—I'm hungry.

PEARL (*crossing to sofa and sitting*). Shut you up, bor, you only just had
lunch.

FRANK. Well I'm hungry again. (*Calling.*) Well, where is this article
we come to see?

BEATIE (*still off*). He ent arrived.

FRANK. Well, he want to hurry 'cos I'm hungry.

BEATIE. You're always hungry.

FRANK. What do you say he is—a strong socialist?

BEATIE. Yes.

FRANK. And a Jew boy?

BEATIE. Yes.

FRANK (*to himself*). Well, that's a queer mixture then.

PEARL (*calling*). I hope he don't talk politics all the time.

FRANK (*examining contents of table*). Have you had a letter from him yet?

PEARL. Stop it, Frank, you know she hevn't heard.

FRANK. Well that's a rum boy friend what don't write. (*Looks at
paintings, pauses before one of them and growls.*)

PEARL. Watch out or it'll bite you back.

(BEATIE *enters* U.L., *she is dressed in her new frock and looks
happy, healthy and radiant.*)

FRANK. Hail there, sister! I was then contemplating your masterpiece.

BEATIE. Well don't contemplate too long 'cos you aren't hevin' it.

FRANK. Blust! I'd set my ole heart on it.

PEARL. That's a nice frock, Beatie.

FRANK. Where's the rest of our mighty clan?

BEATIE. Jenny and Jimmy should be here soon and Susie and Stan
mightn't come.

FRANK. What's wrong wi' them?

BEATIE. Don't talk to me about it 'cos I hed enough! Susie won't
talk to Mother.

PEARL. That make nearly eighteen months she hevn't spoke.

BEATIE. Why ever did you and Mother fall out, Pearl?

FRANK (*sits in armchair* U.L. *of fireplace*). Cos Mother's so bloody stubborn, that's why.

PEARL. Because one day she said she wanted to change her Labour
Tote man, that's why, and she asked me to do it for her. So I said
all right, but it'll take a couple of weeks; and then she get riled
because she said I didn't want to change it for her. And then I ask
her why she didn't change him herself and she say because she was
too ill to go all the way to see John Clayton to tell him, and then
she say to me, why, don't you think I'm ill? And I say—I know
this were tactless o' me—but I say, no Mother, you don't look ill to
me. And she didn't speak to me since. I only hope she don't snub
me this afternoon.

BEATIE (above table). Well, she tell me a different story.

FRANK. Mother's always quarrelling. Blust, she hevn't spoke to her
own mother for three years, not since Granny Dykes took Jenny
in when she had that illegitimate gal Daphne.

BEATIE. Hell! What a bloody family!

FRANK. A mighty clan I say.

(JIMMY and JENNY BEALES now enter U.R.)

JENNY. Hello Frankie, hello Pearl, hello Beatie.

FRANK. And more of the mighty clan.

JENNY (crosses to armchair R. of fire). Mighty clan you say? Mighty
bloody daft you mean. Well, where is he?

FRANK. The mysterious stranger has not yet come—we await.

JENNY. Well, I aren't waitin' long 'cos I'm hungry.

PEARL. That's all this family of Bryants ever do is think o' their guts.

FRANK (to JIMMY). Have you formed your association yit?

JENNY. What association is this?

FRANK. What! Hevn't he told you?

JIMMY (sitting R. of table). Shut you up Frank Bryant, or you'll get me hung.

FRANK. Oh, a mighty association—a mighty one! I'll tell ye. One day
you see we was all sittin' round in the pub—Jimmy, me, Starkie,
Johnny Oats and Bonky Dawson—we'd hed a few drinks and
Jimmy was feelin'—well, he was feelin'—you know what, the itch!
He hed the itch! He started complaining about ham, ham ham all
time. So then Bonky Dawson say, blast, he say, there must be
women about who feel the same. And Starkie he say, well 'course
there are, only how do you tell? And then we was all quiet awhile
thinkin' on it when suddenly Jimmy says, we ought to start an
association of them as need a bit now and then and we all ought to
wear a badge, he say, and when you see a woman wearin' a badge
you know she need a bit, too.

JIMMY. Now that's enough Frank or I'll hit you over the skull.

FRANK. Now, not content wi' just that ole Jimmy then say, and we ought to have a pass word to indicate how bad off you are. So listen what he suggest. He suggest you go up to any one o' these women what's wearin' a badge and you say, how many lumps of sugar do you take in your tea? And if she say "two" then you know she ent too badly off, but she's willin'. But if she say "four" then you know she's in as bad a state as what you are, see?

(*Pause.*)

JENNY. He'd hev a fit if she said she took sixteen lumps though, wouldn't he?

(*Pause.*)

PEARL. Where's mother Bryant?

BEATIE (*looking out of window*). Upstairs changin'.

PEARL. Where's father Bryant?

BEATIE. Tendin' the pigs.

FRANK. You're lucky to hev my presence, you know.

BEATIE. Oh?

FRANK. A little more sun and I'd've bin gettin' in the harvest.

PEARL. Well, what did you think of that storm last night? All that thunder'n lightnin' and it didn't stop once.

BEATIE. Ronnie love it you, know. He sit and watch it for bloody hours.

FRANK. He's a queer article then.

JENNY. He do sound a rumun', don't he?

BEATIE. Well you'll soon see.

JIMMY. Hev he got any sisters?

BEATIE. One married and she live not far from here.

PEARL. She live in the country? A town girl? Whatever for?

BEATIE. Her husband make furniture by hand.

PEARL. Can't he do that in London.

BEATIE. Ronnie say they think London's an inhuman place.

JIMMY. So 'tis, so 'tis!

BEATIE. Here come father Bryant.

(MR. BRYANT *enters from* U.R. *He is in denims and raincoat, tired and stooped slightly.*)

FRANK. And this be the male head of the mighty Bryant clan!

MR. BRYANT. Blust, you're all here soon then.

BEATIE. Get you changed quick Father—he'll be along any minute look.

MR. BRYANT. Shut you up, gal, I'll go when I'm ready. I don't want you pushin' me.

(Mrs. BRYANT *comes from* U.L. *She looks neat and also wears a flowered frock.*)

FRANK. And this be the female head o' the mighty Bryant clan!

MRS. BRYANT. Come on Bryant, get you changed—we're all ready, look.

MR. BRYANT. Blust, there go the other one. Who is he, this boy? That's what I wanna know.

MRS. BRYANT. He's upset! I can see it! I can tell it in his voice. Come on, Bryants, what's the matters?

MR. BRYANT. There ent much up wi' me, what you on about, woman? (*Makes to go.*) Now leave me be, you want me changed look.

MRS. BRYANT. If there ent much up wi' you, I'll marry some other.

FRANK. Healey bin at you, Pop?

BEATIE. The pigs dyin'?

MRS. BRYANT. It's something serious or he wouldn't be so happy lookin'.

MR. BRYANT. I bin put on casual labour.

JENNY. Well, isn't that a cod now!

MRS. BRYANT. Your guts, I suppose.

MR. BRYANT. I tell him it's no odds, that there's no pain. That don't matters, Jack, he says, I aren't hevin' you break up completely on me. You go on casual, he say, and if you gets better you can come on to the pigs again.

MRS. BRYANT. That's half pay then?

BEATIE. Can't you get another job?

FRANK. He've bin wi' them for eighteen years.

BEATIE. But you must be able to do something else—what about cowman again?

MR. BRYANT. Bill Waddington do that, see. He've bin at it this last six'n half years.

JENNY. It's no good upsettin' yourself, Beatie. It happen all the time, gal.

JIMMY. Well, we told her when she was at ours, didn't we?

MRS. BRYANT (*to* MR. BRYANT). All right, get you on up, there ent nothin' we can do. We'll worry on it later. We always manage. It's gettin' late look.

MR. BRYANT. Can he swim? Cos he bloody need to. It's rainin' fit to drowned you. (*Goes off* U.L.)

MRS. BRYANT. Well, shall we have a little cup o' tea while we're waitin'? I'll go put the kettle on. (*Goes to kitchen* U.R.)

(BEATIE *crosses and sits by* PEARL. JENNY *takes out some knitting and* JIMMY *picks up a paper to read. There is a silence. It is not an awkward silence, just a conversationless room.*)

PEARL (*to* JENNY). Who's lookin' after your children?

JENNY. Ole mother Mann next door.

PEARL. Poor ole dear. How's she feelin' now?

JENNY. She took it bad. (*Nodding to* JIMMY.) Him too. He think he
were to blame.

PEARL. Blust, that weren't his fault. Don't be so daft, Jimmy Beales.
Don't you go fretting yourself or you'll make us all feel queer look.
You done nothin' wrong, bor—he weren't far off dying 'sides.

FRANK. They weren't even married, were they?

JENNY. No, they never were—she started lookin' after him when he
had that first stroke and she just stayed.

JIMMY. Lost her job 'cos of it, too.

FRANK. Well, yes, she would, wouldn't she—she was a State Registered
Nurse or something, weren't she? (*To* BEATIE.) Soon ever the
authorities got to hear o' that they told her to pack up livin' wi' him
or quit her job, see?

JENNY. Bloody daft I reckon. What difference it make whether she
married him or not?

PEARL. I reckon you miss him, Jenny?

JENNY. Hell yes—that I do. He were a good ole bor—always joking
and buying the kid sweets. Well, do you know I cry when I heard
it? I did. Blust, that fair shook me—that it did, there!

JIMMY. Who's lookin' after your kid then, Pearl?

PEARL. Father.

(*Pause.*)

JIMMY (*to* FRANK). Who do you think'll win today?

FRANK. Well Norwich won't.

JIMMY. No.

(*Pause.* MRS. BRYANT *enters and sits down above table.*)

MRS. BRYANT. Well, the kettle's on.

PEARL (*to* BEATIE). Hev his sister got any children?

BEATIE. Two boys.

JIMMY. She wanna change her diet then they'll hev girls.

JENNY. Oh shut you up, Jimmy Beales.

MRS. BRYANT. Hed another little win last night.

JENNY. When was this?

MRS. BRYANT. The firemen's whist drive. Won seven'n six in the
knockout.

JENNY. Yerp.

FRANK (*reading the paper*). I see that boy what assaulted the ole woman in London got six years.

MRS. BRYANT. Blust! He need to! I'd've given him six years and a bit more. Bloody ole hooligans. Do you give me a chance to pass sentence and I'd soon clear the streets of crime, that I would. Yes, that I would.

BEATIE (*springing into activity and running into kitchen*). All right, Mother —we'll give you a chance. (*Returning with* JIMMY's *hat and umbrella. Places hat on Mother's head and umbrella in her arms.*) There you are, you're a judge. Now sum up and pass judgement.

MRS. BRYANT. I'd put him in prison for life.

FRANK. You gotta sum up though. Blust, you just can't stick a man in prison and say nothing.

MRS. BRYANT. Good-bye, I'd say.

BEATIE. Come on, Mother, speak up. You sit there and you say you'd clear the streets o' crime an' I hear you pass judgement all the time, now you do it in the proper way. Anybody can say "go to prison" but you want to be a judge. Well, you show a judge's understanding. Talk!

> (*Everyone leans forward eagerly to hear Mother talk. She looks startled and speechless.*)

MRS. BRYANT. Well I—I—yes I—well I—Oh, don't be so soft.

FRANK. The mighty head is silent.

BEATIE. Well yes, she would be, wouldn't she?

MRS. BRYANT. What do you mean, I would be? You don't expect me to know what they say in courts, do you? I aren't no judge.

BEATIE. Then why do you say what you do? Suddenly—out of the blue—a judgement! You don't think about it. If someone do something wrong you don't stop and think why, you just sit and pass easy judgement. No discussin', no questions, just (*Snap of fingers.*) —off with his head. Look, Mother, when something go wrong in the family, do you ever sit and discuss it? I mean look at Father getting less money. I don't see the family sittin' together and discussin' it. It's a problem! But which of you said it concerns you?

MRS. BRYANT. Nor don't it concern them. I aren't hevin people mix in my matters.

BEATIE. But they aren't just people—they're your family, for hell's sake!

Mrs. Bryant. No matters, I aren't hevin' it!

Beatie. But Mother, I—

Mrs. Bryant. Now shut you up, Beatie Bryant, and leave it alone. I
shall talk when I hev to and I never shall do so there!

Beatie. You're so stubborn.

Mrs. Bryant. So you keep saying.

> (Mr. Bryant *enters, he is clean and dressed in blue pin-striped*
> *suit.*)

Mr. Bryant. You brewed up yit?

Mrs. Bryant (*jumping up and going to kitchen, taking hat and umbrella*).
Oh hell, yes—I forgot the tea look.

Mr. Bryant (*sitting above table*). Well, now we're all waitin' on him.

Jenny. Don't look as if Susie's comin'.

Beatie (*up to window*). Stubborn cow!

> (*Silence.*)

Jenny. Hev you seen Susie's television set yit?

Beatie. I seen it.

Frank. Did you know also that when they first hed it they took it
up to bed wi' them and lay in bed wi' a dish of chocolate biscuits?

Pearl. But now they don't bother—they say they've had it a year now
and all the old programmes they saw in the beginning they're seein'
again.

Mrs. Bryant (*entering with tray of teacups and saucers which she hands
round*). Brew's up!

Beatie. Oh, for Christ's sake let's stop gossiping.

Pearl. I aren't gossiping. I'm makin' an intelligent observation about
the state of television, now then.

Mr. Bryant. What's up wi' you now?

Beatie. You weren't doin' nothin' o' the sort—you was gossiping.

Pearl. Well that's a heap sight better'n quotin' all the time.

Beatie. I don't quote all the time, I just tell you what Ronnie say.

Frank. Take it easy, gal—he's comin' soon—don't need to go all
jumpin' an' frantic.

Beatie. Listen! Let me set you a problem.

Jimmy. Here we go.

Beatie (*moving* c. *and taking command*). While we're waitin' for him
I'll set you a moral problem. You know what a moral problem is?
It's a problem about right and wrong. I'll get you bastards thinking
if it's the last thing I do. Now listen. There are four huts.

Frank. What?

BEATIE. Huts. You know—them little things you live in. Now there are two huts on one side of a stream and two huts on the other side. On one side live a girl in one hut and a wise man in the other. On the other side live Tom in one hut and Archie in the other. Also there's a ferryman what run a boat across the river. Now—listen, concentrate—the girl loves Archie but Archie don't love the girl. And Tom love the girl but the girl don't go much on Tom.

JIMMY. Poor beggar.

BEATIE. One day the girl hears that Archie—who don't love her remember—is going to America, so she decides to try once more to persuade him to take her with him. So listen what she do. She go to the ferryman and ask him to take her across. The ferryman say, I will, but you must take off all your clothes.

MRS. BRYANT (*sitting* L. *of table*). Well, whatever do he wanna ask that for?

BEATIE. It don't matters why—he do! Now the girl doesn't know what to do so she ask the wise man for advice, and he say, you must do what you think best.

FRANK. Well that weren't much advice was it!

BEATIE. No matters—he give it. So the girl thinks about it and being so in love she decides to strip.

PEARL. Oh I say!

MR. BRYANT. Well, this is a rum ole story, ent it?

BEATIE. Shut up, Father, and listen. Now-er—where was I?

MR. BRYANT. She was strippin'.

BEATIE. Oh yes! So, the girl strips and the ferryman takes her over— he don't touch her or nothing—just takes her over and she rushes to Archie's hut to implore him to take her with him and to declare her love again. Now Archie promises to take her with him and so she sleeps with him the night. But when she wake up in the morning he've gone. She's left alone. So she go across to Tom and explain her plight and ask for help. But soon ever he knowed what she've done, he chuck her out, see? So there she is. Poor little gal. Left with no clothes and no friends and no hope of staying alive. Now— this is the question, think about, don't answer quick—who is the person most responsible for her plight?

JIMMY. Well, can't she get back?

BEATIE. No, she can't do anything. She's finished. She've hed it! Now, who's to blame?

(*There is a general air of thought for the moment and* BEATIE *looks triumphant and pleased with herself.*)

MRS. BRYANT. Be you a drinkin' on your tea look. Don't you worry about no naked gals. The gal won't get cold but the tea will.

PEARL. Well I say the girl's most responsible.

BEATIE. Why?

PEARL. Well, she made the choice, didn't she?

FRANK. Yes, but the old ferryman made her take off her clothes.

PEARL. But she didn't hev to.

FRANK. Blust woman, she were in love!

BEATIE. Good ole Frank.

JENNY. Hell if I know.

BEATIE. Jimmy?

JIMMY. Don't ask me, gal—I follow decisions, I aren't makin' none.

BEATIE. Father?

MR. BRYANT. I don't know what you're on about.

BEATIE. Mother?

MRS. BRYANT. Drink you your tea, gal—never you mind what I think.

PEARL. What do Ronnie say?

BEATIE. He say the gal is responsible only for makin' the decison to strip off and go across and that she do that because she's in love. After that she's the victim of two phoney men—one who don't love her but take advantage of her and one who say he love her but don't love her enough to help her, and that the man who say he love her but don't do nothin' to help her is most responsible because he were the last one she could turn to.

JENNY. He've got it all worked out then!

BEATIE (*jumping on a chair she thrusts her fists into the air like Ronnie and glories in what is the beginning of a hysteric outburst of his quotes*). "No one do that bad that you can't forgive them."

PEARL. He's sure of himself then?

BEATIE. "We can't be sure of everything but certain basic things we must be sure about or we'll die."

FRANK. He think everyone is gonna listen then?

BEATIE. "People must listen. It's no good talking to the converted. Everyone must argue and think or they will stagnate and rot and the rot will spread."

JENNY. Hark at that then.

BEATIE (*her strange excitement grows. She has a quote for everything*). "If wanting the best things in life means being a snob then, glory hallelujah, I'm a snob. But I'm not a snob, Beatie, I just believe in human dignity and tolerance and co-operation and equality and—"

JIMMY (*jumping up in terror*). He's a communist!

BEATIE. "I'm a socialist!"

MRS. BRYANT. Seems to me as though he ent very happy.

BEATIE. "When I'm with people and I'm singing then I'm happy—when I run away and forget them I'm depressed."

MR. BRYANT (*also using a quoting voice*). And when his backside itch he's in agony!

(*There is a knock on the front door and* JIMMY *subsides back on to his chair.*)

BEATIE (*jumping down from chair joyously as though her excited quotes have been leading to this one moment*). He's here, he's here! (*She goes off* U.L. *but it is only the postman and she returns with a letter and a parcel.*) Oh the fool, the silly fool. Trust him to write a letter on the day he's coming. Parcel for you, Mother.

PEARL. Oh, that'll be your dress from the club.

MRS. BRYANT. What dress is this then? I didn't ask for no dress from the club.

PEARL. Yes, you did, you did ask me, didn't she ask me, Frank? Why, we were looking through the book together, Mother.

MRS. BRYANT. No matters what we was doin' together I aren't hevin' it.

PEARL. But, Mother, you distinctly—

MRS. BRYANT. I aren't hevin' it so there now!

(BEATIE *has read the letter—the contents stun her and she gasps bringing her hand to her mouth. She cannot move. She stares around speechlessly at everyone.*)

Well, what's the matter wi' you, gal? Let's have a read. (*Takes letter and reads contents in a dead flat but loud voice—as though it were a proclamation.*) "My dear Beatie. It wouldn't really work, would it? My ideas about handing on a new kind of life to people are quite useless and romantic if I'm really honest. Perhaps I am asking too much of you. If I were a healthy human being it might have been all right but most of us intellectuals are pretty sick and neurotic—as you have often observed—and we couldn't build a world even if we were given the reins of government—not yet, any rate. This is depressing, and I just don't know what went wrong. I don't blame you for being stubborn, I don't blame you for ignoring every suggestion I ever made—I only blame myself for encouraging you to believe we could make a go of it. We've had precious moments together. But now two weeks of your not being here has given me the cowardly chance to think about it and decide and I—"

BEATIE (*screaming and snatching letter*). Shut up!

MRS. BRYANT. Oh—so we know now, do we?

MR. BRYANT. What's this then—ent he comin'?

MRS. BRYANT. Yes, we know now.

MR. BRYANT. Ent he comin', I ask?

BEATIE (*shouting*). No, he ent comin'.

> (*An awful silence ensues. Everyone looks uncomfortable.*)

JENNY (*softly*). Well blust, gal, didn't you know this was going to happen?

> (BEATIE *shakes her head.*)

MRS. BRYANT. So we're stubborn, are we?

JENNY. Shut you up, Mother, the girl's upset.

MRS. BRYANT. Well I can see that, I can see that, he ent coming, I can see that, and we're here like bloody fools, I can see that.

PEARL. Well, did you quarrel all that much, Beatie?

BEATIE (*as if discovering this for the first time*). He always wanted me to help him but I never could. Once he tried to teach me to type but soon ever I made a mistake I'd give up. I'd give up every time! I couldn't bear making mistakes. I don't know why but I couldn't bear making mistakes.

MRS. BRYANT. Oh—so we're hearin' the other side o' the story now, are we?

BEATIE. He used to suggest I start to copy real objects on to my paintings instead of only abstracts and I never took heed.

MRS. BRYANT. Oh, so you never took heed.

JENNY. Shut you up, I say.

BEATIE. He gimme a book sometimes and I never bothered to read it.

FRANK (*not maliciously*). What about all this discussion we heard of?

BEATIE. I never discussed things. He used to beg me to discuss things but I never saw the point on it.

PEARL. And he got riled because o' that?

BEATIE (*trying to understand*). I didn't have any patience.

MRS. BRYANT. Now it's coming out.

BEATIE. I couldn't help him—I never knew patience. Once he looked at me with terrified eyes and said "we've been together for three years but you don't know who I am or what I'm trying to say—and you don't care, do you?"

MRS. BRYANT. And there she was tellin' me.

BEATIE. I never knew what he wanted—I didn't think it mattered.

MR. BRYANT. And there she were gettin' us to solve that moral problem and now we know she didn't even do it herself. That's a rumun, ent it?

MRS. BRYANT. The apple don't fall far from the tree—that it don't.

BEATIE (*moving to L. of* MR. BRYANT, *wearily*). So you're proud on it? You sit there smug and you're proud that a daughter of yours wasn't able to help her boy friend? Look at you. All of you. You can't say anything. You can't even help you own flesh and blood. Your daughter's bin ditched. It's your problem as well, isn't it? I'm part of your family, aren't I? Well, help me then! Give me words of comfort! Talk to me—for God's sake, someone, talk to me. (*She moves away* U.S. *and cries at last.*)

MR. BRYANT. Well, what do we do now?

MRS. BRYANT (*rising*). We sit down and we eat, that's what we do now.

JENNY. Don't be soft, Mother, we can't leave the girl crying like that.

MRS. BRYANT (*standing behind her chair*). Well, blust, 't'ent my fault she's cryin'. I did what I could—I prepared all this food, I'd've treated him as my own son if he'd come but he heven't! We got a whole family gathering specially to greet him, all on us look, but he heven't come. So what am I supposed to do?

BEATIE (*moving quickly to L. of* MRS. BRYANT). My God, Mother, I hate you—the only thing I ever wanted and I weren't able to keep him, I didn't know how. I hate you, I hate . . .

(MRS. BRYANT *slaps* BEATIE'S *face. Everyone is a little shocked at this harsh treatment.*)

MRS. BRYANT. There! I hed enough!

MR. BRYANT. Well, what d'you wanna do that for?

MRS. BRYANT. I hed enough. All this time she've bin home she've bin tellin' me I didn't do this and I didn't do that and I heven't understood half what she've said and I've hed enough. She talk about bein' part o' the family but she've never lived at home since she've left school look. Then she go away from here and fill her head wi' high class squit and then it turn out she don't understand any on it herself. It turn out she do just the same things she say I do. (*Into* BEATIE'S *face.*) Well, am I right, gal? I'm right, ent I? When you tell me I was stubborn, what you mean was that he told you you was stubborn—eh? When you tell me I don't understand you mean you don't understand, isn't it? When you tell me I don't make no effort you mean you don't make no effort. Well, what you blaming me for? Blaming me all the time! I haven't bin responsible for you since you left home—you bin on your own. All right so I am a bloody fool—all right! So I know it! A whole two weeks I've bin told it. Well, so then I can't help you, my gal, no that I can't, and you get used to that once and for all.

BEATIE. No you can't, Mother, I know you can't.

MRS. BRYANT. I suppose doin' all those things for him weren't enough. I suppose he weren't satisfied wi' goodness only.

BEATIE. Oh, what's the use?

MRS. BRYANT. Well, don't you sit there an' sigh gal like you was Lady Nevershit. I ask you something. Answer me. You do the talking then. Go on—you say you know something we don't so you do the talking. Talk—go on, talk gal.

BEATIE (*to door* U.R., *despairingly*). I can't, Mother, you're right—the apple don't fall far from the tree, do it? You're right, I'm like you. Stubborn, empty, wi' no tools for livin'. I got no roots in nothing. I come from a family o' farm labourers yet I ent got no roots—just like town people—just a mass o' nothin'.

FRANK. Roots, gal? What do you mean, roots?

BEATIE (*quickly down to* R. *of* FRANKIE, *impatiently*). Roots, roots, roots! Hell, Frankie, you're in the fields all day, you should know about growing things. Roots! The things you come from, the things that feed you. The things that make you proud of yourself—roots!

MR. BRYANT. You got a family, ent you?

BEATIE. I am not talking about family roots—I mean—the—I mean— Look! Ever since it begun the world's bin growin', hasn't it? Things hev happened, things have bin discovered, people have bin thinking and improving and inventing but what do we know about it all?

JIMMY. What is she on about?

BEATIE (*various interjections from all*). What do you mean what am I on about? I'm talking! Listen to me! (*The noise fades and slowly the words begin to flow.*) I'm tellin' you that the world's bin growing for two thousand years and we heven't noticed it. I'm telling you that we don't know what we are or where we come from. I'm telling you something's cut us off from the beginning. I'm telling you we've got no roots. Blimey Joe! We've all got large allotments, we all grow things around us so we should know about roots. You know how to keep your flowers alive, don't you, Mother? Jimmy—

you know how to keep the roots of your vegies strong and healthy.
It's not only the corn that need strong roots you know, it's us too.
But what've we got? Go on, tell me, what've we got? We don't
know where we push up from and we don't bother neither.

PEARL. Well, I aren't grumblin'.

BEATIE. You say you aren't—oh yes, you say so, but look at you.
What've you done since you come in? Hev you said anythin'?
I mean really said or done anything to show you're alive? Alive!
Blust, what do it mean? Do you know what it mean? Any of you?
Shall I tell you what Susie said when I went and saw her? She say
she don't care if that ole atom bomb drop and she die—that's what
she say. And you know why she say it? I'll tell you why, because
if she had to care she'd have to do something about it and she find
that too much effort. Yes she do. She can't be bothered—she's
too bored with it all. That's what we all are—we're all too bored.

MRS. BRYANT. Blust woman—bored you say, bored? You say Susie's
bored, with a radio and television an' that? I go t'hell if she's bored!

BEATIE. Oh yes, we turn on a radio or a TV set maybe, or we go to
the pictures—if them's love stories or gangsters—but isn't that the
easiest way out? Anything so long as we don't have to make an
effort. Well, am I right? You know I'm right. Education ent only
books and music—it's asking questions, all the time. There are
millions of us, all over the country and no one, not one of us, is
asking questions, we're all taking the easiest way out. Everyone
I ever worked with took the easiest way out. We don't fight for
anything, we're so mentally lazy we might as well be dead. Blust,
we are dead! And you know what Ronnie say sometimes? He
say it serves us right! That's what he say—it's our own bloody
fault!

JIMMY. So that's us summed up then—so we know where we are then!

MRS. BRYANT. Well if he don't reckon we count for nothin', then it's
as well he didn't come. There! It's as well he didn't come.

BEATIE. Oh, he thinks we count all right—living in mystic communion
with nature. Living in mystic bloody communion with nature,
indeed. But us count? Count, Mother. I wonder. Do we? Do you
think we really count? You don' wanna take any notice of what
them ole papers say about the workers bein' all important these
days—that's all squit! Cos we aren't. Do you think when the
really talented people in the country get to work they get to work
for us? Hell if they do! Do you think they don't know we 'ont

R.–E

make the effort? The writers don't write thinkin' we can understand, nor the painters don't paint expecting us to be interested—
that they don't nor don't the composers give out music thinking
we can appreciate it. "Blust" they say, "the masses is too stupid
for us to come down to them. Blust" they say, "if they don't make
no effort why should we bother?" So you know who come along?
The slop singers and the pop writers and the film makers and
women's magazines and the Sunday papers and the picture strip
love stories—that's who come along, and you don't have to make
no effort for them, it come easy. "We know where the money lie"
they say, "hell we do! The workers've got it so let's give them
what they want. If they want slop songs and film idols we'll give
'em that then. If they want words of one syllable, we'll give 'em
that then. If they want the third rate, blust! We'll give 'em that
then. (*Moving* u.s. *with her back to them.*) Anything's good enough
for them 'cos they don't ask for no more!" The whole stinkin'
commercial world insults us and we don't care a damn. Well,
Ronnie's right—it's our own bloody fault. We want the third rate
we got it! We got it! We got it! We . . .
> (*Suddenly* BEATIE *stops as if listening to herself. She pauses,
> turns with an ecstatic smile on her face.*)

D'you hear that? D'you hear it? Did you listen to me? I'm talking.
Jenny, Frankie, Mother—I'm not quoting no more.

MRS. BRYANT (*resuming her seat at table*). Oh hell, I hed enough of her—
let her talk a while she'll soon get fed up.
> (*The others join her at the table and proceed to eat and murmur.
> When they have settled* BEATIE *moves slowly* D.S. *as though a vision
> were revealed to her.*)

BEATIE. God in heaven, Ronnie! It does work, it's happening to me,
I can feel it's happened, I'm beginning, on my own two feet—I'm
beginning . . .
> *The murmur of the family at the table grows as* BEATIE's *last
> cry is heard. Whatever she will do they will continue to live as before
> and as* BÉATIE *stands alone, articulate at last,*

THE CURTAIN SLOWLY FALLS.

PROPERTY LIST

ACT I

ON STAGE

Clothes line with washing L.

U.S. Pillow case, shirt, face cloth, jersey, pillow case, vest, table cloth
D.S.

D.L. *by fireplace*

Push chair with babies things scattered about (i.e. broken doll, shawl etc.)

By side of push chair building bricks

D.R.

Sacking, oil, spare parts of motor bike in tin

D.S.C.

Toy box and Wellington boots

In front of hearth

Dust pan and brush

On mantelpiece

Candle in saucer

Box of matches

Gaiters (JIMMY)

In hearth

Hob with kettle

On fire guard

Three assorted rags

In oven

Loaf of plaited bread

On left end of sofa

Large pile of magazines with comics on top, cushion covering them

Coat (JIMMY)

Under sofa

Large pile of papers and magazines

On top of U.S. *oven*

Large black saucepan

On table centre

Bottle of sauce

Salt and pepper

Three-quarters of a sliced loaf

Three sets of cutlery (knives, forks and spoons)

Over table on hook

Tilly lamp (battery operated)

On back of U.S. *chair*

Old brown jacket

On back of D.S.R. *chair*

Waistcoat

On draining board extension

Assorted old rags

Tea cloth

Duster

Plate rack with dressings

Large black saucepan

Wire tray (for loaf)

On draining board

Assorted empty milk bottles

Tea cloth

Three soup plates upside down and dinner plate on top

Carton of soap powder

One large dinner plate

Three small plates

Four knives

Two forks

Two spoons

Basin with strawberry and vanilla ice cream

Dessert spoon in ice cream basin

Dish cloth

Large serving spoon

Two teaspoons

In sink

Washing up basin with water

Three small plates round outside of basin

Under draining board
    Pig bucket

On stove
    Frying pan with liver and onions
    and fish slice
    Saucepan with mashed potatoes

In stove
    Two dinner plates (large)

In porch
    Reap hook on pegs
    Broom

P.S. *of porch*
    Empty milk bottle

On chest of drawers
    Washing basket. In it: washing
    with old blue jacket half way
    down
    D.S. basket: shirt

In chest of drawers
    On top shelf L.S.:
        Old pair grey trousers
        Old brown overcoat
        Old waistcoat
        Pair Wellingtons ⎫
        Tennis racket   ⎬ to fall out
        Tins   ⎭
        Three shirts
        Pillow case
    L.S.:
        Jar of sweets
        Bits and pieces of tatt
    Top R. drawer:
        Tray of cutlery
        Dressings
    Top L. drawer:
        Sharpening stone

On table D.S.R.
    Sewing machine with piece of rag
    Sewing basket of bottom shelf

OFF STAGE
    Bicycle (JIMMY)

ACT II, SCENE I

ON STAGE
    Chair U.S. table pulled out

On cooker
    Kettle with hot water
    Small saucepan with lid (potatoes
    in)

Inside cooker
    Casserole with contents (stew)

On table by arm chair
    Wireless
    Bottle with stomach powder
    Tumbler with teaspoon

On mantelpiece
    Clock
    Paper weight
    Matches
    Post cards

Above mantelpiece
    Calendar

By hearth
    Teapot (full)

In copper
    One empty bucket (large)
    One bucket with hot water

On sink unit
    Three large plates
    Seven knives
    Three forks
    Three large serving spoons
    Cup and saucer
    Mug
    Two teaspoons
    Two pudding basins
    Fork in one basin
    Two eggs in mixing bowl
    Jug of water
    Sugar basin with spoon
    Saucepan lid with mashed
    potatoes and fork
    Saucepan with carrots
    Two small towels
    Three small plates
    Large salt jar
    Matches
    Large serving spoon
    Potatoes and peelings
    Mustard in cup and spoon

Under sink
 Dust pan and brush
 Washing up bowl
 Pig bucket
 Two empty buckets
 Newspaper and firewood
 Box of carrots and potatoes
 Damp cloth

On table centre
 "Daily Mail"

On chair left
 "Daily Express"

On exterior wall O.P.
 Tin bath

On copper
 Matches

On table centre
 Chenille cloth
 Table cloth
 False table top
 Table cloth

D.L.
 Water tub. D.S. of it: bucket
 (empty)

OFF STAGE

Off right
 Suitcase
 In it:
  Wrapped apron
  Bath cubes
  Sponge bag
  Dressing-gown
  Red towel
  Dress and hanger

Off left (in front room)
 Record player
 Record on top
 Two paintings with brown paper

Larder U.S.C.
 Milk jug
 Two canisters
 Margarine
 Loaf of bread on plate
 Jar of jam
 Old curtain for bath scene

Four table mats
Check mirror on flat for BEATIE

Off U.L.
 Bicycle

ACT II, SCENE II

STRIKE:
 False table top

SET:
 Three dirty plates
 Three knives, forks and spoons
 Coat on back of door D.C.R.

ACT III

ON STAGE
 Check coat rack off U.L. door
 One or two tier cake stand
 Table laid for meal with dessert
 spoon U.S. centre

On chair R. *end of table*
 Tea cosy

On chair left of fireplace
 "Daily Mirror"

Over fireplace
 Largest of BEATIE's paintings

On bookcase L.
 Magazine

On fireplace
 Large clock
 Four china vases
 Photograph
 Postcards

On table U.R.
 Geranium plant

On bookcase
 Two geranium plants

On window L.
 Plants

OFF STAGE
 Off U.R.
  Large trifle bowl
  Pot of tea
 Off U.L.
  Letter and parcel

PERSONAL PROPERTIES

STAN MANN
    Handkerchief

JENNY BEALES
    Glasses
    Box of matches
    Two hairpins

MR. BRYANT
    Cigarette papers
    Tobacco
    Two cigarettes
    Box of matches
      (all in tin)

PEARL
    Knitting and bag

MUSIC FOR THE SONG

I'LL WAIT FOR YOU IN HEAVENS BLUE

[p. 36]

NOTES

THIS is a play about Norfolk people and it is important that some attempt is made to find out how they talk. A very definite accent and intonation exists and this is not difficult to know.

The following may be of great help:

When the word "wont" is used, the "w" is left out. It sounds the same but the "w" is lost.

Double "ee" is pronounced "i" as in "it"—so that "been" becomes "bin"; "seen" becomes "sin", etc.

"Have" and "had" become "hev" and "hed" as in "head".

"Ing" loses the "g" so that it becomes "in".

"Boy" is a common handle and is pronounced "bor" to sound like "bore".

Instead of the word "of" they say "on" e.g. "I've hed enough on it" or "what do you think on it?"

Their "yes" is used all the time and sounds like "year" with a "p" —"yearp". (Though spelt in manuscript as "yerp".)

"Blast" is also common usage and is pronounced "blust", a short sharp sound as in "gust".

The cockney "ain't" becomes "ent"—also short and sharp.

The "t" in "what" and "that" is left out to give "thaas" and "whaas". e.g. "Whaas matter then?"

And other idiosyncracies are indicated in the play itself.